Glossary

PASS PERFECT

Series 7 Glossary

Numerical

10K report   the annual audited financial statements of corporate issuers that are filed with the SEC, and which are a public record. Included in the 10K are the corporation's balance sheet; income statement; retained earnings statement; and sources and uses of cash statement.

12-b-1 plan   named after the SEC rule, a plan which allows mutual funds, under strictly controlled circumstances, to charge their shareholders for the fund's advertising expenses and costs associated with attracting new investors.

13D report   a report filed with the SEC by anyone who accumulates a 5% or greater holding in a publicly traded company, this is a public announcement that this person may intend to exercise "control" over the corporation, or may attempt to take over the company.

401(k) plan   a corporate pension plan to which an employee contributes a defined percentage of his or her salary via payroll deduction up to a maximum dollar amount. These contributions are made with pre-tax dollars. In some cases, the employer will match each employee's contribution to the plan up to a certain percentage. A 401(k) plan with this feature is sometimes called a matching plan.

403(b) plan   a pension plan specifically for certain tax-exempt, non-profit organizations - e.g., schools, universities, hospitals, etc. - to which an employee contributes a defined percentage to a tax-deferred annuity or mutual fund via payroll deduction. The amount contributed is always made with pre-tax dollars and is therefore a salary reduction for the employee.

529 (b) plan   a state-sponsored education savings plan that allows non-tax deductible contributions to be made to a trust to pay for a beneficiary's qualified higher education expenses. Maximum annual contributions and funding are set by each state. Earnings build tax deferred and distributions to pay for qualified higher education expenses are not taxable.

8K report   a corporate filing made with the SEC for any unusual events that occur, such as a declaration of a merger, divestiture, bankruptcy, or change in the composition of the Board of Directors of the corporation.

A

Accelerated depreciation a deduction taken from income to reflect the "using up" over time of a fixed asset such as machinery or buildings. Accelerated depreciation methods allow for larger deductions in the earlier years of an asset's life; compensated for by smaller deductions in the later years of an asset's life. In aggregate, the total deduction over the asset's life is the cost of the asset. (compare Straight line depreciation)

Accommodation liquidation also known as a "Cabinet Trade," a procedure on the CBOE that allows options contract holders and writers to liquidate worthless contracts at an aggregate premium of $1.00.

Account executive also known as a broker or registered representative, an individual who is employed by a broker-dealer to handle customer accounts and to advise the public about investing in securities. This person must be registered with a self-regulatory organization such as FINRA and licensed with a Series 7, or other appropriate license.

Accounts receivable turnover ratio the ratio of annual sales to year end accounts receivable for a company. This measures how quickly the sales made by the company (which are booked at the sale date, with collection to occur later) are being collected by the company.

Accredited investor under Regulation D, a purchaser of a private placement who has a net worth of at least $1,000,000; or an annual income of at least $200,000 for the past two years (or a couple with joint annual income of $300,000); or an officer of director of the issuer; or is an institution, such as a pension fund or insurance company. (see Regulation D)

Accretion the annual earning, taken as income, of a portion of the discount on a bond purchased below par, as that bond's value increases towards par as it approaches maturity. Each year, the accretion amount is shown as interest income earned; and the bond's cost basis is adjusted upwards towards par by that accretion amount. Note that there is both accretion for tax purposes, as defined by IRS rules; and accretion for book purposes, as defined by FASB (Financial Accounting Standards Board rules). (compare Amortization)

Accrued interest the amount of interest that builds up between semi-annual interest payments on a bond. This amount must be paid from buyer to seller on settlement date of a bond trade. For corporate, municipal, and agency bonds, accrued interest is calculated based on an arbitrary 30-day month and 360-day year. For U.S. Government securities, accrued interest is calculated based on the actual days of each month and the actual number of days in the year. (compare Flat bond)

Accumulation account an account established by the sponsor of a fixed unit investment trust to accumulate bond positions that will be subsequently formally transferred into a trust, and sold to investors as trust units that represent an undivided interest in the trust portfolio.

Accumulation units the legal name for the "shares" that a customer acquires in the separate account when purchasing a variable annuity, since this is a "unit" trust form of investment company. The dividends and capital gains received during the investment period are reinvested in the separate account, purchasing additional accumulation units. (see Separate account, Annuity units)

Acid test a slang term for a company's "Quick" ratio, since the ratio is based upon the company's assets that are quickly convertible into cash - this is the ratio of all current assets minus inventories and prepaid expenses to all current liabilities. This is a liquidity measure that is a more stringent test than the Current ratio. (compare Current ratio)

Acquisition   in investment banking, the purchase of a smaller company by a larger company. Investment bankers advise both the buyer and seller in such transactions. Usually, the acquisition is made at a premium to that company's current market price - which serves as an inducement for the Board of Directors of the targeted company to approve the acquisition. Payment can be made in either cash; or in the stock of the acquiring company.

Active asset management   the pursuit of investment returns in excess of the specific benchmark return. Active asset managers believe that undervalued stocks exist in the marketplace, and that by investing in them, they can surpass the performance of a similar index fund. (compare Passive asset management)

Active return   the excess return achieved by an asset manager above the specified benchmark (compare Passive return)

Ad valorem taxes   the formal name for property taxes (which are based upon property value, hence the name "ad valorem" (Latin for "to the value") that back a municipal general obligation (G.O.) bond. (see General obligation bond)

Additional bonds test   1) for corporate bonds, a pledge not to issue additional bonds unless there is sufficient collateral value backing the issuance of the new bonds (see Mortgage bond); 2) for municipal revenue bonds, a pledge not to issue additional bonds unless there are sufficient revenues backing the issuance of the new bonds.

Additional paid in capital   also called capital surplus or capital in excess of par value, the amount above par value paid for the common shares by an investor on the initial public offering.

Additional takedown   that portion of the total takedown on a municipal bond new issue that a syndicate member receives when a selling group member sells a bond. (see Total takedown, Selling concession)

Adjustable rate debt   a debt security whose interest rate is reset periodically (e.g., semi-annually, annually) to reflect current interest rates, as determined by a formula specified in the bond's trust indenture. Unlike fixed rate debt, whose price moves inversely with market interest rate movements; the interest rate on adjustable rate debt changes with market interest rates, hence the price stays at par.

Adjustable rate preferred (ARP)   a preferred stock whose dividend is adjusted periodically to reflect interest rate changes. The rate may change monthly, quarterly, or annually. Usually the rate is set to the highest of either a selected Treasury Bill or Treasury Bond rate. Unlike fixed rate preferred, whose price moves inversely with market interest rate movements; the dividend rate on adjustable rate preferred changes with market interest rates, hence the price stays at par.

Adjustment bond   also known as an income bond, this debt security pays interest only if the company earns the interest or to the extent that the company earns the interest. These are usually issued by a corporation trying to reorganize its capitalization in order to avoid bankruptcy. With the existing bondholders' approval, the corporation exchanges its regular bonds for adjustment bonds, where the interest rate or par value is adjusted upwards; however the new bonds pay interest only if the corporation has sufficient earnings (thus, these are also known as "income bonds"). Adjustment bonds trade flat, that is, without accrued interest.

ADR   commonly used abbreviation for American Depositary Receipt. These are negotiable securities representing ownership of the common or preferred stock of a foreign company that is being held in trust. The securities of the foreign company are deposited in a foreign branch of an American bank. Receipts (ADRs) are issued against this deposit which entitle the ADR holder to receive all the dividends and to participate in the capital appreciation of the foreign company's securities. The number of ADRs issued against the shares on deposit may or may not be on a one-for-one basis. ADRs are perhaps the easiest and most popular way for Americans to invest in the securities of foreign companies. Another name for these securities is American Depositary Shares (ADSs).

ADS   commonly used abbreviation of American Depositary Share. These are negotiable securities representing ownership of the common or preferred stock of a foreign company that is being held in trust. The securities of the foreign company are deposited in a foreign branch of an American bank. Receipts are issued against this deposit which entitle the ADS holder to receive all the dividends and to participate in the capital appreciation of the foreign company's securities. The number of ADSs issued against the shares on deposit may or may not be on a one-for-one basis. ADSs are perhaps the easiest and most popular way for Americans to invest in the securities of foreign companies. Another name for these securities is American Depositary Receipts (ADRs).

Advance / Decline ratio   the ratio of the number of stock issues advancing in price on a given trading day versus the number of stock issues falling in price on that day. This ratio gives an indication of the "strength" of any market move, and is a measure of the "breadth" of the market.

Advance refunding   when interest rates have dropped, a municipal issuer who has sold bonds that are non-callable, can issue new bonds with a lower coupon rate and use the proceeds to buy other bonds (usually U.S. Government securities which are placed in escrow). The income from the escrowed U.S. Governments pays the interest on the older high rate outstanding municipal debt and when the U.S. Government securities mature, the proceeds are used to retire the old, outstanding municipal issue. In effect, the issuer is prepaying both interest and principal on the old bonds with the escrowed U.S. Government securities - thus these bonds are "advance refunded" and no longer have a claim on the issuer's taxing power or revenues. Advance refunding allows the issuer to reduce its interest cost on a non-callable issue when interest rates have fallen. (see Defeasance; Pre-refunding)

Affiliated person   a definition under Rule 144, an affiliated person is anyone who is controlled by the seller of securities under Rule 144. Rule 144 limits sales of restricted and control securities, either by the seller or any "affiliated persons."

Age Weighting   the ongoing reallocation of funds in a portfolio as a customer ages. In the customer's younger years, the portfolio is weighted more towards growth. In the customer's older years, the portfolio is re-weighted more towards income and safety.

Agency notes   debt securities with one or two years to maturity that are issued as a source of interim financing by U.S. Government agencies such as the Federal Home Loan Bank, the Federal National Mortgage Association, etc.

Agency securities   also called Federal agency securities, these are securities issued by agencies of the U.S. Government. These agencies include the Government National Mortgage Association (GNMA), Federal National Mortgage Association (FNMA), Federal Home Loan Mortgage Corporation (FHLMC), Federal Farm Credit Banks, Student Loan Marketing Administration (SLMA), Tennessee Valley Authority (TVA), and the World Bank. Except for Government National Mortgage Association (GNMA) securities, these securities are not direct obligations of the U.S. Government.

Agency transaction   a trade where the executing member acted as a middleman or broker, finding the person in the market with the lowest price for a customer who wishes to buy; or the person in the market with the highest price for a customer who wishes to sell. In agency transactions, the executing member earns a commission for finding the "best market" for the customer. Also, a member firm may be an agent in an underwriting when it does not take financial liability for the issue, such as in a "best efforts" underwriting. (compare Principal transaction)

Agent   a registered person or business organization that acts as the intermediary in the purchase or sale of a security and charges a commission for the service. A broker, registered representative or account executive is an agent. A brokerage firm may be an agent in an underwriting when it does not take financial liability for the issue, such as in a "best efforts" underwriting. (see Account executive)

Agreement among underwriters   more often called the syndicate agreement, a formal, legal agreement between the syndicate manager and each syndicate member that details the selling responsibility (including allocation of securities) and liability of each syndicate member in the underwriting of a new issue security. Such agreements can either be established as "Eastern" syndicate accounts (undivided as to selling responsibility and liability); or "Western" syndicate accounts (divided as to selling responsibility and liability). (see Syndicate, compare Underwriting agreement, Eastern syndicate, Western syndicate)

AIR   abbreviation for "Assumed Interest Rate," the annual rate of return used in the prospectus of variable annuity that illustrates the compounding effect of contributions over the life of the contract and the resultant value of the annuity at retirement. The AIR is conservatively presented for illustrative purposes only; it is not a guaranteed rate of return.

All or none   1) abbreviated AON on an order ticket, a notation on a contingency order instructing the floor broker to execute the entire order at one price at one time. Depending on the time limit on the order, the floor broker can repeatedly attempt to execute the order; (compare Fill or kill); 2) a best efforts underwriting commitment that is contingent upon the sale of the entire issue. (see All-or-none commitment); 3) a dealer offering of securities where the entire block must be purchased at the offered price; a partial sale will not be permitted.

All or none commitment   a type of best efforts underwriting commitment in which the investment banker agrees to complete the terms of the underwriting agreement if, and only if, the entire new issue sells out. If it is not entirely sold, then the underwriting is canceled and all monies are returned to any investor who bought the issue. (see Best efforts commitment)

Allied Member   a New York Stock Exchange license designation for a partner or principal in a FINRA/NYSE member firm that is qualified to supervise all firm activities.

Alpha   a measure of a stock's price movement relative to the stocks in its industry and independent of general market movements. A stock with a high "alpha" moves faster than the average of the stocks in its grouping; a stock with a low "alpha" moves slower than the average of the stocks in its grouping. (compare Beta)

Alternative minimum tax   an alternate tax computation that must be used by persons who have reduced their regular taxable income excessively by relying on so-called "tax preferences." Sometimes called the "tax on tax preferences," this is a flat 26%-28% tax rate that is applied to income, adjusted upwards by the preference items that the taxpayer used to reduce his or her regular tax liability excessively. Tax preference items include: 1) accelerated depreciation amounts in excess of straight line; 2) excess percentage depletion deductions; 3) excess intangible drilling cost deductions, and; 4) interest income from non-essential private purpose municipal bonds, such as Industrial development bonds.

AMBAC   acronym for American Municipal Bond Assurance Corp., one of the private companies that insure the timely payment of interest and principal on a municipal bond issue. This "insurance," for which the municipality pays a fee, results in a better credit rating, and therefore a lower interest cost, for the issuer. (see MBIA, FGIC, BIGI)

American depositary receipts (ADRs)   commonly known as ADRs, these are negotiable securities representing ownership of the common or preferred stock of a foreign company that is being held in trust. The securities of the company are deposited in a foreign branch of an American bank. Receipts (ADRs) are issued against this deposit which entitle the ADR holder to receive all the dividends and to participate in the capital appreciation of the foreign company's securities.

The number of ADRs issued against the shares on deposit may or may not be on a one-for-one basis. ADRs are perhaps the easiest and most popular way for Americans to invest in the securities of foreign companies. Another name for these securities is American Depositary Shares (ADSs).

American depositary shares commonly known as ADSs, these are negotiable securities representing ownership of the common or preferred stock of a foreign company that is being held in trust. The securities of the company are deposited in a foreign branch of an American bank. Receipts are issued against this deposit which entitle the ADS holder to receive all the dividends and to participate in the capital appreciation of the foreign company's securities. The number of ADSs issued against the shares on deposit may or may not be on a one-for-one basis. ADSs are perhaps the easiest and most popular way for Americans to invest in the securities of foreign companies. Another name for these securities is American Depositary Receipts (ADRs). (see American Depositary Receipts)

American Stock Exchange an auction trading market with a trading floor located in lower Manhattan for smaller and mid-size companies, commonly known as the AMEX. The AMEX also trades listed options, and is the principal market trading ETFs - Exchange Traded Funds.

American-style option a call or put option that can be exercised at any point from the time it is purchased until its expiration. (compare European style option)

AMEX the abbreviation for the American Stock Exchange, an auction trading market with a trading floor located in lower Manhattan for smaller and mid-size companies. The AMEX also trades listed options, and is the principal market trading ETFs - Exchange Traded Funds.

Amortization an annual non-cash expense reflecting the annual decline in value of a premium bond towards par value as the bond approaches maturity. The annual amortization amount is both a reduction of interest income reported; and an annual reduction to the cost basis of the bond. Note that there is amortization for tax purposes, as defined by IRS rules; and amortization for book purposes, as defined by FASB (Financial Accounting Standards Board) rules. (compare Accretion)

AMT bonds abbreviated name for non-essential use, private purpose municipal revenue bonds that are subject to the Alternative Minimum Tax. (see Alternative minimum tax)

And interest   a synonym for a debt instrument trading with accrued interest. (see Accrued Interest; compare Flat bond)

Annual report   an abbreviated version of Form 10K which all public companies are required by the SEC to print and distribute to their shareholders annually. The annual report contains audited financial statements as well as other information about the company's performance and business plans. (see Form 10K)

Annuitization   the conversion of accumulation units to a fixed number of annuity units by the insurance company that issued the variable annuity contract. Annuitization occurs when the investor is ready to begin receiving payments from the annuity at retirement.

Annuity   an investment contract, typically issued by an insurance company, into which the purchaser (known as the annuitant) makes regular or lump sum payments for a period of time and begins receiving regular distributions at a fixed date in the future. The distribution of payments typically begins at retirement and the annuitant chooses the payout option (e.g., life annuity; life annuity period certain). If the amount of the periodic payment that will eventually be made to the annuitant is fixed, then the contract is known as a fixed annuity. If the amount of the annuitant's payment will vary with the value of the securities underlying the contract, then it is called a variable annuity. (see Fixed annuity; Variable annuity)

Annuity units   the fixed number of units upon which the pay-out from a fixed or variable annuity is calculated. The number of annuity units is fixed when the accumulation units are annuitized. (compare Accumulation units)

Anti-dilutive covenant   a covenant associated with a convertible security that enables the holder to maintain the right to convert to the same percentage of outstanding shares following a new issue of common stock, a stock dividend, or a stock split. Under the covenant, the company increases the security's conversion ratio (and lowers the conversion price) proportionate to the amount of newly issued securities when any of these events occur. (see Dilution)

AON 1) abbreviation for "All or None." An AON order specifies that the order be filled in its entirety; if not the order cannot be filled, but later execution attempts are permitted (compare FOK, IOC); 2) AON also is used in when dealers offer securities. If a security is offered in a dealer listing as AON, then the entire block must be purchased at the offered price; purchase of part of the issue is not permitted.

Appreciation an increase in the value of an asset held for investment. (compare Depreciation)

Arbitrage 1) the simultaneous purchase and sale of the same security in different markets in an attempt to profit from short-term price disparities between the two markets; 2) the simultaneous purchase of a convertible security; and sale of the common stock into which the security is convertible; to profit from a short-term price disparity that may exist in the market between these two "equivalent" securities.

Arbitrage account an account in which an investor performs arbitrage transactions or sells "short against the box." In such transactions, the customer has equal long and short positions, and has no credit risk (one side exactly offsets the other). Because of this, the margin requirement is quite low. Currently, the New York Stock Exchange sets the margin for these transactions at 5% of the market value of the long side. (see Short against the box)

Ascending yield curve a graph of the yields of fixed income securities of the same type (e.g., U.S. Governments or Corporates or Municipals) by maturity. As the maturity lengthens, the yield increases, so the curve "ascends." This is a normal yield curve shape, showing that investors will accept lower yields for shorter maturities; but demand higher yields for longer maturities (since there is greater risk). (compare Inverted (Descending) yield curve, Flat yield curve)

Ask price 1) also known as the offer price or asked price, this is the best price at which a market maker or dealer offers to sell a security to a buyer; 2) for mutual funds, the Public Offering Price of the fund shares to anyone who wishes to buy. (compare Bid price)

Asset   on a balance sheet, any item owned by a company that can be exchanged for cash or has value. (see Current asset, Fixed asset, Intangible asset)

Asset allocation   the systematic and thoughtful placement of investment dollars into various classes of investments such as stocks, bonds, and cash equivalents. (see Asset class)

Asset class   the categorization of investments into groupings with similar risk and return characteristics, i.e., money market instruments are an asset class, long term corporate bonds are an asset class, large capitalization common stocks are an asset class, etc.

Assignment   the signature of the seller on a stock or bond certificate, transferring ownership to the new buyer in return for payment.

Assumed interest rate   the annual rate of return used in the prospectus of variable annuity that illustrates the compounding effect of contributions over the life of the contract and the resultant value of the annuity at retirement. The AIR is conservatively presented for illustrative purposes only; it is not a guaranteed rate of return.

At the close   a notation placed on an order instructing the floor broker on the exchange floor to execute the order in the final 30 seconds of the market - during the ringing of the closing bell. An "at the close" order is to be executed at the closing price or canceled. (compare At the open)

At the money   for option contracts, when the market price of the underlying security and the option's strike price are the same. Thus, there is no profit or loss on the contract (disregarding any premium paid or received). (compare In the money, Out the money)

At the open   a notation placed on an order instructing the floor broker to execute the order in the opening price range when a security begins trading. The order is automatically canceled if it is not executed at that time. (compare At the close)

Auction market a phrase used to describe how "open outcry" trading is performed on a stock exchange. In reality the exchange is a "double" auction market in which buyers call out successively higher bids and sellers call out successively lower offers until a trade is arranged at a price satisfactory to both parties. (compare Negotiated market)

Auction rate preferred preferred stock whose dividend is adjusted periodically by the issuer; however, the shareholders (usually large corporations) must agree to the rate before it goes into effect. If they do not, the issuer continues to offer better rates until one is accepted; or will repurchase all the securities. (see Adjustable rate preferred)

Authorized shares the maximum number of common or preferred shares that a corporation is permitted to issue in its Articles of Incorporation. Typically, a company does not issue all of its authorized shares during the initial public offering. A company may increase the number of authorized shares by amending its Articles of Incorporation; however, the amendment must be approved by a majority vote of the outstanding shares.

Authorizing resolution the document adopted by a municipal issuer that exercises its power to issue securities. The municipal issuer is given the authority to do so under the enabling provisions of the State constitution, statutes, charters and ordinances.

Average life for serial bonds, which mature over a sequence of years, the number of years to the point at which half of the principal on the outstanding bonds has been paid off. The formula for computing the average life of an issue is the total bond years divided by the total number of bonds issued, assuming each bond has a $1,000 par value. (see Bond year)

Averaging down a strategy through which an investor lowers the average price paid for each share of stock by purchasing more shares when the price declines.

B

Baby bond   a bond with a face or principal value of less than $1000, usually $100. Such bonds are issued when the issuer wishes to attract very small investors.

Back-end load   a fee that is charged when an investor redeems mutual fund shares. (see Contingent deferred sales charge)

Backing away   a prohibited practice, this occurs when a securities dealer gives a firm quote and then refuses to trade at that quote.

Balance of payments deficit or surplus   the relative level of sales of goods and services to foreign countries by the United States; versus purchases of goods and services from foreign countries by the United States. A balance of payments surplus means that the U.S. is exporting more than it is importing; a balance of payments deficit means that the U.S. is importing more than it is exporting.

Balance sheet   a snapshot of a company's financial position that shows all of its assets, liabilities, and net worth (stockholder's equity). On a balance sheet, the total assets (current, fixed, and intangibles) must equal the total liabilities (current and long-term) plus the net worth. (compare Income statement)

Balance sheet formula   the formula net worth, restated for presentation in a balance sheet. The formula for Net Worth is: Assets - Liabilities. Restated for the balance sheet, this becomes: Assets = Liabilities + Net Worth.

Balanced fund   a management company that invests in common stocks for growth; and preferred stocks and bonds for income: to achieve a "balance" of both.

Balloon maturity   a feature of a bond with serial maturities in which an unusually large amount of an issue matures at one time. The balloon usually occurs in the later years of the issue's sequence of maturity dates. (see Serial bond)

Bank-qualified municipal bond   a municipal G.O. issue of $10,000,000 or less which, if purchased only by a bank investor, allows the bank to deduct 80% of the interest it pays on the deposits used to purchase the bonds. The interest income received from the bonds is tax free to the bank.

Banker's acceptance (BA)   a money market instrument that is a time draft used to finance international trade. A bank issues a draft payable at face amount to the seller of the goods at a future date (typically 30 - 90 days in the future; the time that it takes to ship the goods to their destination). This draft can be traded at a discount to the face amount. The difference between the discount price and the face value is the interest on the banker's acceptance.

Banks for Cooperatives   part of the Federal Farm Credit Consolidated System, this agency makes seasonal and term loans solely to cooperatives owned by farmers. (see Federal Farm Credit Consolidated System)

Basis   the yield to maturity on a bond. (see Yield to maturity)

Basis point   one basis point equals .01% on a bond or 1/100 of a 1% yield change per $1,000 par value bond. Each basis point therefore equals $.10 of interest per year. If the yield on a bond changes from 6.50% to 6.75%, this is a change of 25 basis points or a total dollar change of $2.50 (25 basis points x $.10) per $1,000 par value bond.

Basis quote   a synonym for a yield-to-maturity quote. (see Yield-to-maturity)

Bear call spread the sale of a lower strike price call option; and the purchase of a higher strike price call option; on the same underlying security. This is a bear market strategy, also termed a Short Call Spread. In a falling market, both calls expire "out the money." There is a profit from the net premium credit received. Spreads are gain-limiting and loss-limiting positions. (compare Bull call spread)

Bear market a period during which the overall prices of securities are declining. (compare Bull market)

Bear put spread the purchase of a higher strike price put option; and the sale of a lower strike price put option; on the same underlying security. This is a bear market strategy, also termed a Long Put Spread. In a falling market, the long put with the higher strike goes "in the money" first for a profit. If the market keeps dropping, the lower strike price short put also goes "in the money," limiting potential gain to the difference in the strike prices (net of the premium paid). Spreads are gain-limiting and loss-limiting positions. (compare Bull Put Spread)

Bear spread an option strategy involving buying and selling calls simultaneously on the same stock or buying and selling puts simultaneously on the same stock in anticipation of a decrease in the price of the underlying stock.

A Bear call spread is the sale of a lower strike price call option; and the purchase of a higher strike price call option; on the same underlying security. This is a bear market strategy, also termed a Short Call Spread. In a falling market, both calls expire "out the money." There is a profit from the net premium credit received.

A Bear put spread is the purchase of a higher strike price put option; and the sale of a lower strike price put option; on the same underlying security. This is a bear market strategy, also termed a Long Put Spread. In a falling market, the long put with the higher strike goes "in the money" first for a profit. If the market keeps dropping, the lower strike price short put also goes "in the money," limiting potential gain to the difference in the strike prices (net of the premium paid).

Bearer bond   a fully negotiable, unregistered bond with bearer coupons attached. Neither the bondholder's name nor the principal amount are registered with the issuer - both are payable to the "bearer." The person owning the bond must clip and present the coupons on the assigned dates in order to receive the interest payments; and must present the "corpus" (par value certificate) of the bond to receive the final principal payment. Such bonds can no longer be issued in the United States, but are issued overseas. (compare Registered bond)

Bell shaped yield curve   an unusual yield curve shape that looks like a "bell shape," also called a hump shaped yield curve. In such a yield curve, yields for medium term maturities are higher than yields for both short term and longer term issues. This indicates a demand-supply imbalance in the medium term issues (their yields are higher than longer term issues due to lack or demand for; or an oversupply of; the medium term issues). (see Yield curve; compare Ascending yield curve, Inverted yield curve)

Bellwether security   a security that is a leading indicator of the overall movement of the market or of a specific segment, such as bonds. For example, historically, the bellwether Treasury bond issue is the 30-year bond.

Beneficial owner   term for the investor who actually owns securities held in street name in a margin account. (see Street name)

Best efforts commitment   a type of underwriting commitment in which the underwriter, acting as an agent, agrees to sell an issuer's new securities to the public on demand. Any amount of the securities that remain unsold is returned to the issuer. The underwriter, therefore, assumes no financial liability if the security cannot be sold to the public. (compare Firm commitment)

Best market   in the Over-The-Counter market, the highest bid price and lowest ask price for a security. This is the "inside market" and represents the best prices at which the security can be traded.

Beta   also called the Beta coefficient, the relative volatility of a particular stock relative to the overall market as measured by the Standard & Poor's 500 index. If a stock's Beta coefficient is +1, this means that its price rises and falls in direct relationship to the movement of the index. A Beta that is less than +1 indicates a stock is less volatile than the overall market; while a Beta of greater than +1 indicates that a stock is more volatile. A - Beta indicates that the stock's price moves in the opposite direction to the market as a whole. (compare Alpha)

Bid form   in a competitive bid underwriting of a new issue municipal bond, the form on which an underwriting syndicate submits its bid to the issuing municipality. The form includes the coupon rates proposed by the underwriter and the price at which the underwriter proposes to purchase the new bonds from the issuer (typically par, though a small premium or discount from par may be allowed). The bidder with the lowest interest cost to the issuer wins. (see Bidding syndicate)

Bid price   1) the best price at which a market maker or dealer will buy a security from a customer who wishes to sell; 2) for mutual funds, the Net Asset Value (NAV), which is the price at which the fund will redeem shares of customers who wish to sell. (compare Ask price)

Bidding syndicate   for a competitive bid underwriting of a new issue municipal bond, the group of underwriters that formulates and submits a bid for a municipal new issue. (see Competitive municipal bid)

Bids wanted   abbreviated by "BW" in dealer listings such as the Pink Sheets, Yellow Sheets, or OTCBB, this shows that the dealer has securities for which he is soliciting a bid from any interested buyers. (compare Offers Wanted)

Big Board stocks   a popular name for stocks that trade on the New York Stock Exchange, the "biggest" of the stock exchanges in terms of market capitalization.

BIGI   acronym for Bond Investors Guaranty Insurance Corp., a private company that insures the timely payment of interest and principal on a bond issue. This "insurance," for which the municipality pays a premium, results in a better credit rating and therefore lower interest costs for the issuer. (see AMBAC, MBIA, FGIC)

Blanket bond   insurance that broker-dealers are required to carry in order to cover losses due to illegal incidents such as theft or securities forgery. It is also known as a blanket fidelity bond and it is not a security. (see Fidelity bond)

Blind pool   a direct participation program limited partnership in which the objectives of the pool are stated, but the specific investments are not yet selected at the time that the partnership is formed.

Block   a large amount of stocks or bonds that is being held or traded. Usually, a block of stock is 10,000 shares or more of the same issue. A block of bonds has a face value of $200,000 or more. On the ticker, the entire amount of a block trade is shown followed by the symbol s. (see S)

Block positioning   when a broker-dealer uses its own funds to buy a large block of securities into its own inventory from a large customer who wishes to sell. This benefits the customer, who wishes to be paid in full for selling the large block, as opposed to selling the issue piecemeal into the market. The broker-dealer assumes the market risk of the price of the issue dropping prior to reselling the position. Large block orders are handled in this way so as not to disrupt the market.

Bloomberg   a financial services information provider similar to Reuters, that gives real time quotes, trade reports, and analytical information on equities and U.S. Government, Agency, Corporate and Municipal debt.

Blue chip stock   a term used to describe securities issued by the most well-established, and consistently profitable American companies. Such companies have a history of steady growth and dividend payments. Investing in these companies is considered to be relatively safe and conservative. The term "blue chip" was adopted from poker, where a blue chip has the highest value.

Blue List   a daily publication listing the prices (yields) of municipal bonds being offered by dealers in the secondary market. It also includes very limited listings of corporate bonds. Subscribed to by other dealers, and not distributed to the general public, this list gets its name from the color of the paper on which it is printed. (Note that the Blue List ceased operations in the fall of 2001, but may still be tested.)

Blue List total   the total, at face value, of all municipal bonds being offered for sale in the secondary market on a given day. This is a technical indicator of the available supply of municipal bonds, published daily in the back section of the Blue List. (Note that the Blue List ceased operations in the fall of 2001, but may still be tested.) (see Blue list)

Blue-sky laws   commonly used name for Uniform Securities Act - the state laws (as opposed to the federal securities laws) that govern the securities industry. The name comes from stock promoters in the early 1900s who would sell investors pieces of the "Blue Sky." The Uniform Securities Act requires the registration of securities, broker-dealers and agents in each state, unless an exemption is available. An account executive or registered representative must take the Series #63 examination to be properly registered in the states that have adopted the Uniform Securities Act.

Board Broker   an options exchange member who handles the book of public limit orders that are "away from" the current market price. (compare Order book official)

Board of directors   individuals elected by a company's shareholders to set the firm's management policies, including determining the amount of the dividend that common shareholders will receive.

Bond   a long-term debt security or IOU issued by a corporation, municipality, or government. The purchaser of this security in the initial public offering, in effect, loans the issuer money. In return, the issuer agrees to pay interest on the loan, either at a fixed or variable rate; and to repay the principal amount (face value) at maturity. Traditionally most bonds pay interest semi-annually. However, zero-coupon bonds do not make such periodic interest payments. (see Zero-coupon bonds)

Bond anticipation note (BAN)   a short-term municipal security issued as a source of interim financing when a long term bond is about to be issued. The proceeds from the issuance of the bonds will be used to retire the BAN. This security typically matures in less than one year and there are no periodic interest payments during this period. The payment at maturity consists of both the repayment of the principal and the interest earned over the life of the security. (compare Construction loan note, Revenue anticipation note, Tax anticipation note, Tax and revenue anticipation note)

Bond appraisal   in the municipal market, an approximation of the value of bonds that a customer wishes to sell. Since the trading market is thin, there is no "real time" price reporting, as for stocks. Therefore, the true market value of the bonds is uncertain. A bond appraisal gives the customer an approximate value for the security.

Bond Buyer   sometimes called The Daily Bond Buyer, the daily newspaper of the municipal bond market which contains articles primarily about the new-issue marketplace and its participants, official notices of sale, bond redemption notices, and statistics about interest rates and trading activity.

Bond Buyer Index   published by the Bond Buyer, the index is the yield of 20 selected general obligation bonds with 20 years to maturity, all rated "A" or better. (compare Revdex)

Bond counsel   also known as the bond attorney, the lawyer or law firm that prepares all the legal documents for a new issue municipal bond (the bond resolution, trust indenture (if there is one) and official statement; and which renders the legal opinion attesting to a bond's legality, validity, and tax-exempt status. (see Legal opinion)

Bond interest coverage ratio   a ratio that measures a company's ability to meet fixed interest charges, it is the ratio of income before paying bond interest expense to bond interest expense.

Bond ratio   the ratio of a company's long term debt to total long term capital. Total long term capital consists of common stockholders' equity, preferred stockholders' equity, and long term debt. Common stockholders' equity consists of common at par + capital in excess of par + retained earnings.

Bond resolution   the contract between the issuer and the bondholder that details all of the covenants ("promises") to which the issuer must adhere in return for the loan from the bondholder.

Bond year   for a serial bond issue that matures over a sequence of years, each one-year period that a $1,000 par value bond is outstanding. The total bond years of a particular maturity is computed by multiplying the number of $1,000 par value bonds in that maturity by the number of years from the bond's dated date to its maturity. (see Average life, Maturity, Dated date.)

Bonded debt   the total debt that a municipality has outstanding including its net direct debt and overlapping debt. This total is used in analyzing the creditworthiness of a municipal general obligation bond. (see Net direct debt, Overlapping debt)

Book entry   term describing securities for which no physical certificates are issued. The names, addresses, and holdings of investors are listed only in the computerized records of the issuer, registrar, or transfer agent.

Book value   1) the theoretical value of the company that remains if all the assets of the company were liquidated at the values carried on the balance sheet; and then all liabilities are paid off with the proceeds. Intangible assets such as goodwill, patents, and copyrights are excluded from total assets, since their "real" value is uncertain if the company were liquidated; 2) for securities, the accounting value used to value the securities on the holder's books; as opposed to the value for tax purposes.

Box   the physical location where securities are held in safekeeping at a brokerage firm. This term comes from the time, many years ago, when firms held the certificates in a large tin box.

Branch Office Manager   a FINRA/NYSE license designation for an individual who has passed the Series #9/10 examination. A Branch Manager is qualified to approve new accounts, transactions in accounts, and can approve correspondence of an individual nature to a customer.

Breadth of the market   a measure of the strength of a market movement, the number of individual stocks whose prices have moved in the same direction as the overall market as measured by a change in the market index. For example, if the Standard and Poor's 500 Average was up by 20 points; with 400 issues advancing and 100 declining; this indicates a strong market move upwards.

Breakeven point   the point at which an investor does not have a profit or loss on an investment.

Breakout   a price rise to, and through, a resistance level that results in a substantial further price advance; or a price decline to, and through, a support level that results in a substantial further price decline. (see Support level, Resistance level)

Breakpoint   the dollar investment levels at which a mutual fund investor qualifies for a lowered sales charge. The larger the dollar amount invested, the lower the sales charge imposed at each breakpoint level. (see Letter of intent)

Broad based index option   an index option contract based on a stock index that includes issuers in many different industries; and/or countries. Examples of broad based index options are the Standard and Poor's 100 Index Option (OEX); and Standard and Poor's 500 index Option (SPX). (compare Narrow based index option)

Broker   1) a registered representative or account executive at an exchange member firm; 2) a member firm that acts as an intermediary, or agent, in a securities transaction.

Broker loan rate   also known as the call loan rate, the interest rate that banks charge brokerage firms for loans collateralized by marketable securities (margin loans). This rate is lower than the prime rate (the rate that banks charge their best business customers for unsecured loans) because marketable securities are placed with the bank as collateral.

Broker's broker   1) a professional trader that acts as agent for institutions that wish to acquire or dispose of large blocks of municipal bonds. By using a broker's broker, the institution keeps its identity undisclosed. Municipal broker's brokers act as agent only; they do not carry an inventory of municipal bonds nor do they underwrite new issues; 2) on the New York Stock Exchange, the Specialist performs the function of a broker's broker when he takes orders that are "away from the market" from retail firms and places them on his book for execution if the market should move to that price. (see Specialist's book)

Brokers wire   a newswire service of J. J. Kenny Drake and Co. which gives information about the municipal marketplace, primarily about issues in the secondary market and general economic information.

Bull call spread   the purchase of a lower strike price call option; and the sale of a higher strike price call option; on the same underlying security. This is a bull market strategy, and is also termed a Long Call Spread. In a rising market, there is a profit on the long call (lower strike) that ultimately is limited by the higher strike short call. Spreads are gain-limiting and loss-limiting positions. (compare Bear call spread)

Bull market   a period during which the overall prices of securities are rising. (compare Bear market)

Bull put spread   the sale of a higher strike price put option; and the purchase of a lower strike price put option; on the same underlying security. This is a bull market strategy, also termed a Short Put Spread. In a rising market, both puts expire "out the money." There is a profit from the net premium credit received. Spreads are gain-limiting and loss-limiting positions. (compare Bear put spread)

Bull spread   an option strategy involving buying and selling calls simultaneously on the same stock or buying and selling puts simultaneously on the same stock in anticipation of an increase in the price of the underlying stock.

A Bull Call Spread is the purchase of a lower strike price call option; and the sale of a higher strike price call option; on the same underlying security. This is a bull market strategy, and is also termed a Long Call Spread. In a rising market, there is a profit on the long call (lower strike) that ultimately is limited by the higher strike short call.

A Bull Put Spread is the sale of a higher strike price put option; and the purchase of a lower strike price put option; on the same underlying security. This is a bull market strategy, also termed a Short Put Spread. In a rising market, both puts expire "out the money." There is a profit from the net premium credit received.

Business cycle   the four stages through which the economy (and business) tend to move. The stages, in their normal order, are: expansion, prosperity, recession, and recovery.

Business risk   the risk that an issuer's business declines, often due to technological change, bad business decisions, and law changes. In turn, the value of that issuer's securities declines.

Butterfly spread a spread involving the purchase of a low strike price option; the purchase of a high strike price option; and the sale of 2 equal middle strike price options. (The 2 middle options are the "body" of the "Butterfly;" the low and high strike price options are the "wings" of the "Butterfly." Please note that these complex spreads are not included on the #7 examination.

Buying power the amount of marginable securities that can be purchased using the SMA available in a margin account. For marginable equity securities, Buying Power is 2 times the SMA amount. (see Special memorandum account)

BW abbreviation for Bids Wanted in dealer listings such as the OTCBB, Pink Sheets, and Yellow Sheets, this shows that the dealer has securities for which he is soliciting a bid from any interested buyers. (compare OW - Offers Wanted)

C

Cabinet trade 1) on the NYSE, exchange-listed companies' stocks (usually preferred stock) that trade infrequently; or stocks that are very highly priced. Such stocks trade in round lots of 10 shares instead of round lots of 100 shares. The securities get their name from the metal racks in which orders for these infrequently traded securities are placed until they are executed or canceled; 2) on the CBOE, a procedure that allows options contract holders and writers to liquidate worthless contracts at an aggregate premium of $1.00.

Calamity call the same as a catastrophe call, under the terms of the call covenant for a municipal bond, the issuer is obligated to call an outstanding issue if the facility backing the bond is accidentally destroyed. The insurance required under the bond's insurance covenant usually provides the money to redeem the issue.

Calendar spread an option spread position, where simultaneously the same type of option is bought and sold with the same strike price; and different expirations. When the positions are "stacked" one above the other, there is a no difference in the strike prices, but the expirations are different - on a time line, one expiration is longer than the other, hence the name calendar spread. These are also called "horizontal" spreads. (compare Vertical spread, Diagonal spread)

Call date the dates (and prices) stated in the bond contract at which the issuer can call in bonds from holders under the terms of an "in whole" call feature or a sinking fund call feature.

Call feature a provision of a bond contract or preferred stock contract that permits the issuer to call in the securities from the holders at a pre-established price prior to maturity. Issuers will call in the securities if interest rates have dropped after issuance, allowing the issuer to refinance at lower current rates. (see In-whole call, Sinking fund call, Catastrophe call; compare Put feature)

Call loan   loans from bank to broker, where marginable securities are the collateral. These are also termed "broker loans." The interest rate charged on these loans is the "call loan rate" or "broker loan rate."

Call loan rate   the interest rate that banks charge brokerage firms for loans collateralized by marketable securities. (see Broker loan rate)

Call option   a contract that gives the holder the right, but not the obligation, to buy a fixed amount of securities (e.g., 100 shares of stock) at a fixed price for a fixed period of time. The holder of the contract has the right to "call away' the security, hence the name. For this right, the holder pays a premium - the market price of the contract. The writer or grantor of a call option is obligated to sell a fixed amount of securities at the fixed price, when, and if, the option is exercised. For granting this right, the writer receives the premium. (compare Put option)

Call premium   the amount above par that an issuer will pay a preferred stockholder or bondholder to call in the security early. (see Call feature)

Call protection   a period of time after the issuance of a callable security when it cannot be called. Most preferred stock and bond issues that are callable offer at least 10 years of "call protection" from the issue date.

Call risk   the risk that an issuer will call outstanding bond or preferred stock issues in periods of falling interest rates.

Callable bond   a bond that the issuer has the option to call, i.e., redeem or retire, before the maturity date. Usually the bond is called at a premium over par value. Issuers will call in bonds when interest rates have dropped, allowing the issuer to refund the issue at lower current rates. (compare Puttable bond)

Callable preferred stock   preferred stock that the issuer has the option to redeem or repurchase at a specified price from the stockholders. Usually, the preferred is called at a premium to its par value. Issuers will call in outstanding preferred shares if interest rates have dropped, allowing the issuer to refinance at lower current rates. Note that common stock is never callable; only preferred stock and bonds can be callable.

Cancel/rebill record   a requirement of FINRA/NYSE, a written record detailing any change of account designation to a customer order or position

Capital appreciation an increase in the market value of a security or the overall market.

Capital gain   the profit that results when the proceeds from the sale of a security are higher than the security's cost basis. (see Sale proceeds, Cost basis)

Capital asset pricing model   sometimes abbreviated "CAPM," a methodology for finding the most efficient investments - those that give the greatest return for the amount of risk assumed. The model identifies the most efficient investments as those that give a rate of return equal to the "risk-free" rate of return (the rate of return for investments only having systematic risk) plus a premium for any non-systematic risk inherent in the investment. (see Systematic risk, Non-systematic risk)

Capital gains (losses)   one of the two types of portfolio income, the gains or losses resulting from the sale of an asset held for investment. Capital gains (or losses) are short term if the security is held for one year or less; and long term if the security is held for more than one year. (see Portfolio income)

Capital in excess of par   also known as capital surplus or additional paid in capital, the amount by which the price paid by a purchaser of the common stock on the initial public offering exceeds the stated par value of the issue.

Capital market instrument   a debt obligation with a maturity longer than one year. This is a source of long term capital for the issuer, hence the name. (compare Money market instrument)

Capital risk   the risk that an investment depreciates and the investment can only be sold at a loss.

Capital stock   any type of equity security used to capitalize a company. In informal usage, the term has come to refer to only common stock, although in actuality it includes preferred stock as well.

Capital surplus   also called capital in excess of par or additional paid in capital, the amount above par value paid for the common shares by a purchaser on the initial public offering.

Capitalization   that part of a company's funds raised by issuing stocks and long-term bonds. This is the long term capital of the company.

Capitalized interest   the cost of borrowing money during the construction phase of a project, this amount is added into the total cost of the project. Businesses can recover this cost when the property is placed into service through the depreciation deductions allowed over the property's life.

Cash account   an account defined under Regulation T, in which an investor buys securities by paying in full; or sells securities that he or she owns fully paid (a long sale of the securities).

Cash assets ratio   the most stringent test of a company's liquidity, this is the ratio of cash to total current assets.

Cash dividends   part of a company's after-tax earnings which its Board of Directors decides, usually quarterly, to distribute to the shareholders.

Cash settlement   a procedure in which a trade settles the same business day by 2:30 PM EST, allowing the seller access to his or her funds more rapidly than in a regular way (3 business day) settlement. (compare Regular way settlement)

Cash-equivalents   short-term investments, such as money market fund shares, that are virtually like cash because of their high-liquidity and safety.

Cashier department   part of a brokerage firm's operations or "back office" that is responsible for handling the actual securities and cash as they are received into and delivered from the firm. This department also handles stock loans to other customers and financial institutions.

Catastrophe call   under the terms of the call covenant for a municipal bond issue, the issuer is obligated to call an outstanding issue if the facility backing the bond is accidentally destroyed. The insurance required under the bond's insurance covenant usually provides the money to redeem the issue (compare In-whole call, Sinking fund call)

CBOE   abbreviation for the Chicago Board Options Exchange, the largest listed options trading market in the United States.

Central Registration Depository   known as "CRD," this is FINRA's database of information on each registered representative, including each registered representative's disciplinary history.

Certificate of accrual on Treasury securities   a product of Salomon Brothers, CATS are, in effect, U.S. Government zero-coupon bonds. Conventional Treasury bonds are deposited with a trustee, "stripped" of coupons, and certificates are issued and sold to investors representing a single principal repayment at maturity. Investors receive no interest payments over the life of the security. The difference between the discounted price and the maturity price is the interest payment. These are commonly known as Treasury Receipts.

Certificate of deposit (CD)   a short-term money market instrument issued by a bank at par that repays principal and interest at maturity.

Certificate of limited partnership   the document, filed with the state, that is a public record of all partners and their percentage interest in a direct participation program. Thus, anyone who wishes to sue the partners can find out who they are!

Charting   capturing the patterns of a stock's price and volume movements on a line, bar, point-and-figure, or moving average graph. So-called "chartists" attempt to fathom the future direction of a stock's price from these patterns. (see Technical analysis)

Chartist   a technical analyst who uses charts to capture a stock's price movement and trading volumes; and then analyzes this information as a basis for making buy and sell recommendations.

Cheap stock rule   an NYSE/NASD (now FINRA) regulation that sets the minimum margin to sell short cheap stocks (those under $5 per share) at the greater of: 100% of the security's market value or $2.50 per share. This high margin reflects the high level of risk of shorting such "cheap" stocks.

Chicago Board Options Exchange   abbreviated as the CBOE, the largest listed options trading market in the United States.

Chicago Mercantile Exchange   a futures market that trades foreign currency futures and options on these futures. This market is regulated by the Commodities Futures Trading Commission (CFTC); not the Securities and Exchange Commission. Futures are not securities; nor are options on futures securities; hence they are not on the securities examinations.

Chinese wall   the term for a "barrier" placed on the flow of information between an investment banking firm's underwriting department or research department and its trading department. The "wall" is established to prevent insider trading abuses by the firm's trading department using information obtained from the underwriting department about possible restructuring or new issue offerings; or obtained from the research department about new recommendations.

Churning   excessive trading in a customer's account by a broker in order to generate commissions. Churning is a prohibited practice.

Circuit breaker   slang for New York Stock Exchange Rule 80B that requires the market to be shut for specified time periods if the market drops by a large amount (currently 10% as measured by the Dow Jones Industrial Average).

Classified stock   1) a stock that is separated into more than one class, i.e., Class A common or Class B common. Usually there are some differences in the rights and privileges granted to various classes; 2) a mutual fund share separated into more than one class, with each class having different sales charges and 12-b-1 fees. Class A shares have an up-front sales charge and low continuing 12-b-1 fees. Class B shares have a contingent-deferred sales charge and higher 12-b-1 fees. Class C shares have a lower contingent-deferred sales charge and the highest 12-b-1 fees. (see 12-b-1 plan; Contingent-deferred sales charge)

Clearing house funds   monies payable upon regular way settlement of a securities transaction at a designated clearing house such as the Depository Trust and Clearing Corporation. Regular way trades of equities, corporate, and municipal bonds settle in clearing house funds, 3 business days after trade date. (compare Federal funds)

Closed-end fund   also called a publicly-traded fund, a type of management company that issues a fixed number of negotiable shares to the public. These shares are not redeemable with the fund, as is the case with an open-end management company, or mutual fund. Such a structure is used for securities portfolios that are illiquid (making redemption difficult) such as emerging markets funds; or municipal bond funds. Closed-end fund shares trade in the secondary market - either on an exchange or OTC - like any other stock. The shares' market price may be at, above, or below the shares' net asset value, depending on investor sentiment towards the fund. (see Publicly traded fund, Closed-end management company; compare Open-end fund)

Closed-end management company   also called a publicly-traded fund, a type of investment company that issues a fixed number of negotiable shares to the public. These shares are not redeemable with the fund, as is the case with an open-end management company, or mutual fund. Such a structure is used for securities portfolios that are illiquid (making redemption difficult) such as emerging markets funds; or municipal bond funds. Closed-end fund shares trade in the secondary market - exchange or OTC - like any other stock. The shares' market price may be at, above, or below the shares' net asset value, depending on investor sentiment towards the fund. (see Publicly traded fund; compare Open-end fund)

Closed-end mortgage bond   a provision in a mortgage bond's trust indenture that prohibits a corporation from issuing additional bonds with the same level of legal claim on the real estate that backs the bond issue. Only bonds with lower (junior) status to already outstanding bonds backed by the same real estate may be issued. (see Mortgage bond; compare Open-end mortgage bond)

Closing purchase   in the options market, when an investor's ending option transaction in a specific contract is a purchase of an option. In such an instance, the investor opened with a sale of an option (an opening sale); and liquidated the "short" position with a closing purchase, buying back that same option. (see Opening sale; compare Opening sale, Closing sale)

Closing sale   in the options market, when an investor's ending option transaction in a specific contract is a sale of an option. In such an instance, the investor opened with a purchase of an option (an opening purchase); and liquidated the "long" position with a closing sale, selling that same option. (see Opening purchase; compare Opening sale, Closing purchase)

CMO   acronym for Collateralized Mortgage Obligation, this is a derivative debt security that is collateralized by a portfolio of GNMA, FNMA, or FHLMC mortgage backed pass-through certificates. The payments from the certificates are allocated into streams of differing maturities called tranches. Each tranch, therefore, behaves like a conventional bond. (see Tranch)

Code of procedure   FINRA/NASD's procedures for hearing customer complaints if the customer has not previously signed an arbitration agreement.

Coincident economic indicator   an economic measure that indicates the economy's current position in the business cycle. Gross National Product (GNP), personal income, and the index of industrial production are among the coincident indicators. (compare Leading economic indicator, Lagging economic indicator)

Collar   in options, a person who has bought stock and then sells a call at a strike price just above the market price of the stock, and buys a put at a strike price just below the market price of the stock. If the stock rises, it is called away; if the stock falls, the put is exercised, limiting downside loss. Because a premium was received and a premium was paid, the cost of the downside protection is often "0."

Collateral trust bond   a secured corporate bond that is backed by marketable securities that a company owns in its investment portfolio. These securities are held by a trustee who protects the investors' interests, and these marketable securities are the "collateral" backing the issue.

Collateralized mortgage obligation (CMO)   a derivative debt security that is collateralized by a portfolio of GNMA, FNMA, or FHLMC mortgage backed pass-through certificates. The payments from the certificates are allocated into streams of differing maturities called tranches. Each tranch, therefore, behaves like a conventional bond. (see Tranch)

Collection ratio   for municipalities, the percentage of taxes assessed that are actually collected by the municipality (some people don't pay their taxes!).

Combination   an option strategy involving either buying a call and a put on the same stock; or selling a call and a put on the same stock, with both options having the different strike prices and/or expiration dates. If an investor buys both the call and the put simultaneously, this is a long combination and the investor expects the price of the stock to move either up or down a limited amount. If an investor sells both the call and the put simultaneously, this is a short combination and the investor expects the price of the stock to remain relatively flat.

Combination oil and gas program   an oil and gas program that combines exploratory, developmental and income programs into one overall "combined" program. (see Exploratory, Developmental, Income oil and gas programs)

Combination order   an order to buy a call and a put; or sell a call and a put; on the same security with different strike prices and/or expirations. Because filling this order requires that two trades be completed at the same time, these orders are given priority on the Chicago Board Options Exchange floor.

Combined margin account   a margin account with both long and short positions. Such an account is treated basically as two separate accounts - a long account and a short account.

Commercial paper   unsecured short-term money market debt issued by a corporation with a maximum maturity of 270 days. Commercial paper is issued at a discount and matures at face value.

Commission   the fee charged by a broker for executing an agency trade for a customer. The commission amount on an agency trade must be disclosed on the customer's confirmation. (compare Mark-up)

Common at par   on a company's balance sheet, the portion of the price paid on the initial public offering by shareholders that equals the stated par value of the shares (this is often set artificially low, since some states tax corporations based on par value). Any price paid for the shares above par value is called additional paid in capital (or capital surplus; or capital in excess of par value).

Common carrier issue   securities issued by railroads, airlines, trucking companies that are subject to regulation by the ICC - Interstate Commerce Commission (now part of the Department of Transportation). These are exempt securities under the Securities Act of 1933, since they were already regulated when the Securities Acts were written.

Common stock   an equity security that gives the owner the right to receive dividends, vote on company issues, and vote for the Board of Directors. The common stockholder is the last person in line whose claims are satisfied should a corporation go bankrupt.

Common stock equivalent   a security that can be converted into common stock. Convertible bonds and convertible preferred stocks are considered common stock equivalents.

Common stock ratio   the ratio of a company's common stockholders' equity to total long term capital. Common stockholders' equity consists of common at par + capital in excess of par + retained earnings. Total long term capital consists of common stockholders' equity, preferred stockholders' equity, and long term debt.

Common stockholder's equity   the portion of a company's long term capital that, in theory, belongs to the common shareholders. Common stockholders' equity includes common at par value, capital in excess of par value and retained earnings.

Companion tranch   a Collateralized Mortgage Obligation tranch associated with a Planned Amortization Class (PAC) tranch that absorbs prepayment risk and extension risk before these affect the PAC tranch. This tranch has the most variable repayment date. (see Collateralized mortgage obligation; compare Planned amortization class)

Comparison   a dealer to dealer confirmation of a trade, listing of all relevant data about the transaction, that a firm's Purchase and Sales department sends to the contra-broker dealer. This information is used to match trades between broker-dealers, so that settlement can occur smoothly. Any unmatched trades must be reconciled by both broker-dealers involved in the trade. (see DK)

Competitive bid auction   a bid placed at the yield auction of U.S. Government securities in which the bidder specifies the interest rate (yield) on the bid. The winning bids are those with the lowest interest rates, representing the lowest interest cost to the U.S. Government. The higher interest rate competitive bids lose, and are not filled. (compare Non-competitive bid)

Competitive bid underwriting used primarily for initial offerings of most municipal general obligation bonds and all U.S. Government debt securities, a type of underwriting in which investment banking firms submit bids in accordance with specifically advertised criteria to the issuer, who then chooses those bids that will result in the lowest interest cost. (compare Negotiated underwriting)

Competitive municipal bid in a competitive bid underwriting of a new issue municipal bond, the specific interest rates at which an underwriting syndicate proposes to buy the offering from the issuer. The lowest interest rate bidder is awarded the issue. The bid to the municipality must be submitted with a good faith check. (see Good faith check)

Competitive trader a registered New York Stock Exchange member who trades solely for his or her own account on the floor of the exchange. The presence of such persons on the exchange floor added liquidity to the market (another person willing to buy or sell always helps!). This type of trader is virtually obsolete, since most trades on the NYSE now occur via SuperDOT or Direct Plus - the exchange's automated trading systems. (compare Floor trader, Specialist)

Compliance officer a FINRA/NYSE designation for an individual who has passed the Series #14 examination. This person is responsible for overall firm compliance, and supervises all Branch Office Managers (Series #9/10 licensed individuals) in that firm.

Compliance Registered Options Principal a Chicago Board Options Exchange license designation for a person who has passed the Series #4 examination. This person is located in a supervisory office and is responsible for insuring the firm's overall compliance with exchange and SEC rules; and for approving communications with the public.

Concession the discount from the public price given to the member of a selling group that is participating in a new issue underwriting. (see Selling concession)

Conduct Rules the body of rules created by FINRA/NASD to govern dealer-customer relations, that require that customers be treated "fairly, justly and equitably."

Confirmation a notice sent from the broker to the customer no later than the day after the trade date that discloses the details of the execution of an order, including price, number of shares, settlement date, and commission.

Conservator for incompetent account another name for a guardian account, the court appoints a conservator to protect the assets of a minor or an incompetent individual.

Consolidated Quotations Service abbreviated as CQS, this service shows bid and ask quotes for NYSE listed issues, from all market makers in these securities, including regional stock exchange Specialists that "dual-list" the stock, and over-the-counter Third Market makers that make a market in that stock. Thus, one can find the best market for NYSE listed issues, no matter where the quote originates.

Consolidated tape an electronic ticker that reports trades of all securities listed on the New York Stock Exchange (called the Network A tape), no matter where the trade took place. Reporting trades to the tape on a real time basis, aside from the NYSE itself, are regional stock exchange Specialists that "dual-list" the stock, and over-the-counter Third Market makers that make a market in that stock. There is also a "Network B" tape for all trades in American Stock Exchange listed issues.

Consolidation a period of price stability in the market, where there is no discernible uptrend or downtrend in prices.

Constant-dollar plan an investment method in which a person maintains a fixed-dollar amount of a portfolio in stocks with any overage being used to buy bonds. If the stock portfolio value drops below the fixed dollar amount, some of the bonds are liquidated, and additional stocks are purchased, to bring the stock portfolio back to the constant dollar amount. (compare Constant ratio plan)

Constant-ratio plan   an investment method in which a person maintains a fixed percentage of the total portfolio value in stocks and a fixed percentage in bonds. Regular adjustments to the balance of the portfolio composition between stocks and bonds are made as values change to keep the ratios constant. (compare Constant dollar plan)

Constitutional debt limit   a limit, expressed as a percentage of assessed valuation, on the dollar amount of bonds that a municipality can have outstanding at any one time.

Construction loan note (CLN)   a municipal debt offering with a two-to-five year maturity whose proceeds are used to finance a large construction project. Upon completion of the facility, the CLN is taken out - i.e., is paid off - using the proceeds from issuing a long term bond. (compare Bond anticipation note, Revenue anticipation note, Tax anticipation note, Tax and revenue anticipation note)

Consumer Confidence Index   a leading economic indicator published by the Conference Board measuring consumer confidence levels, and hence, likely future consumer spending levels.

Contingency order   the group name of limit, stop, and stop-limit orders. Because these orders are placed "away from" a stock's current market price, their execution is contingent upon the market reaching the price specified on the order.

Contingent-deferred sales charge   a mutual fund that does not impose an up front sales charge, but rather, charges a fee if the investor redeems the shares within a relatively short period of time after purchasing them. The fee declines the longer the securities are held. This is also called a "back-end load."

Contra-broker   a term used to describe a broker who takes the other side of a trade.

Contrary indicators information used to establish the bullish or bearish sentiment of the market to which an investor responds by taking the opposite position. For example the level of odd lot purchases and sales is a contrary indicator under the Odd Lot Theory. This theory states that small investors tend to trade odd lots and that they are wrong. Thus, if the small investor is buying odd lots, one would sell; if the small investor is selling odd lots, one would buy.

Control stock stock held by an officer or director of a company, or by a person or family with a controlling interest in the company. Control stock held by officers and directors is most often acquired through company stock option plans. Control stock owned by a person or family is often the founder's stock, or has been inherited by the founder's family members as part of a trust. Sales of control stock in the public market must comply with the requirements of SEC Rule 144. (see Rule 144)

Conversion price the stated price at which a security is convertible into the common stock of the issuer.

Conversion ratio the number of common shares that an investor will receive when converting a bond or preferred stock.

Convertible adjustable preferred stock a preferred stock, whose dividend rate changes periodically based upon changes in market interest rates, and that can be converted into common stock.

Convertible debenture a bond that the holder can convert into a fixed number of common shares. The conversion ratio is set when the bond is issued. (see Subordinated debenture)

Convertible preferred   preferred stock that the shareholder can convert into a fixed number of common shares. The conversion ratio is set when the preferred stock is issued. Note that common stock can never be convertible - only preferred stock and bonds can have a conversion feature.

Convertible security   a "senior" security (senior to common stock as to priority of claim in a liquidation, such as preferred stock or bonds) that allows the holder to convert into a predetermined number of common shares.

Cooling off period   the 20-day period following the filing of a registration statement with the SEC for a new non-exempt securities offering. During the "cooling off" period, the issue cannot be sold, advertised, recommended; nor can orders to buy the issue be solicited from customers. During the "cooling off" period, the SEC reviews the filing for "full and fair disclosure."

Corporate account   an account opened by a corporation to buy and sell securities. Before the account can be opened, the company must complete a resolution authorizing the opening of the account.

Cost basis   1) for tax purposes, the original price paid for a security , inclusive of commissions or mark-ups; 2) The cost basis of discount bonds may have to be accreted for tax purposes; while the cost basis for premium bonds may have to be amortized for tax purposes; 3) When the holder of a call option exercises, buying the stock, the cost basis of the stock for tax purposes is equal to the strike price plus the premium. When the writer of a put is exercised, buying the stock, the cost basis is equal to the strike price minus the premium; 4) For limited partnerships investments, the cost basis is the cash investment plus assumption of recourse debt (and non-recourse debt for real estate only). The partnership investment cost basis must be adjusted each year for additional cash investments or distributions; assumption or paydown of debt; and the distributive share of partnership income and loss.

Cost depletion   an annual non-cash expense deducted for the "using up" of natural resources (e.g., oil, gas, timber) owned by a business. In a direct participation program (DPP), the depletion allowance enables the business to recover the cost of buying the natural resource. The depletion allowance can be computed on a cost or percentage basis. Under cost depletion, the business deducts the actual cost of purchasing the natural resource as it is used up. (compare Percentage depletion)

Counter-cyclical stock   the common stock of companies whose market value and performance move opposite to the phases of the business cycle. Companies that produce basic food products are counter-cyclical because when peoples' income declines, they eat out less and eat in more. (compare Cyclical stock)

Country fund   a management company that invests in the securities of companies located in one country, whose name the fund bears. Emerging market country funds tend to be closed-end funds, since these investments can be highly illiquid. More developed country funds tend to be open-end funds. (see Closed-end fund, Open-end fund)

Coupon bond   another term for a bearer bond, this is a fully negotiable, unregistered bond with bearer coupons attached. Neither the bondholder's name nor the principal amount are registered with the issuer - both are payable to the "bearer." The person owning the bond must clip and present the coupons on the assigned dates in order to receive the interest payments; and must present the "corpus" (par value certificate) of the bond to receive the final principal payment. Such bonds can no longer be issued in the United States, but are issued overseas. (compare Registered bond)

Coupon rate   also known as the stated yield or nominal yield, this is the fixed rate of interest paid on a bond. (see Nominal yield, Stated yield)

Cover   1) the slang term for closing out or liquidating a short position by buying back the shares that have been sold short and delivering them to the lender; 2) in a competitive bid underwriting of a new issue municipal bond, the difference between the winning bid and the next best bid submitted (the next best bid is the "covering bid," and if the winning bidder cannot complete the terms of the contract, the covering bidder is next in line to buy the new issue from the municipality).

Coverdell Education Savings Account previously called an "Education IRA," a tax deferred account that allows a maximum aggregate $2000 non-deductible contribution to be made for the purpose of paying for a child's higher education expenses. (compare IRA, Roth IRA)

Covered option term used to describe a short call or put that is protected against loss by another security position or money position. For example, owning the underlying security or a countervailing option position covers the sale of a call option. Shorting the stock, owning a countervailing option position, or depositing cash equal to the strike price, covers the sale of a put. The term "covered" is only associated with the writer of an option, who is protected against market risk. (see Short call, Short put; compare Naked option)

Covered straddle term used to describe an options strategy where a customer buys the underlying stock and sells both a call and a put with the same terms against the underlying stock position. This is a neutral market strategy for income, that earns double premiums from selling 2 options positions against the long stock position. In reality, only the short call side of the straddle is "covered" by the long stock position; the short put side of the straddle is naked and exposes the customer to loss in a falling market. (see Short straddle)

CRD abbreviation for Central Registration Depository, this is FINRA's database of information on each registered representative, including each registered representative's disciplinary history.

Credit agreement a "truth in lending" statement given by the broker-dealer to the customer when a margin account is opened. This document explains how the margin loan balance is computed and how interest will be charged on the outstanding balance.

Credit balance in a short margin account, the credit received from selling short a security, plus the 50% initial margin deposit required for the short sale. This credit is not released to the customer until the securities have been repurchased and replaced, covering the short position. (compare Debit balance, Free credit balance)

Credit risk   the risk that the issuer of a bond (or preferred stock) may default on interest and principal payments.

Credit spread   an option spread in which the investor simultaneously buys the option with the lower premium and sells the option with the higher premium. The net difference between the lower premium paid and the higher premium received is the credit. This type of spread is profitable if the difference (the "spread") between the premiums narrows or if both options expire. (see Spread; compare Debit spread)

Creditor   a person to whom money is owed. For example, bondholders are creditors of bond issuers.

Cross-over point   as the years progress in a limited partnership, tax deductions decrease and (hopefully) income increases. The point where income increases; and tax deductions decrease; so that the program begins to generate positive taxable income, is the "cross-over" point.

Crossing   a securities transaction in which an OTC trader executes a buy order and a sell order in the same stock from different customers at the current market price, in effect offsetting one order against the other. The broker earns a commission on both sides of transactions. Crossing is also permitted on the CBOE floor, if the floor broker first attempts to fill each side in the market prior to matching the customer buy and sell orders. Crossing is prohibited on the NYSE. Crossing is always prohibited at prices away from a stock's current market price.

CTR   acronym for a Currency Transaction Report, which is required to be filed with FinCEN (Financial Crimes Enforcement Network) for receipts and disbursements of more than $10,000 in cash.

Cum-rights   literally "with" rights, this term describes transactions in which preemptive rights that have been issued by the company to existing shareholders accompany the purchase (or sale) of that common stock and their value is included in the market price of the shares. (see Preemptive right; compare Ex rights)

Cumulative preferred   if a company misses its dividend payments, holders of cumulative preferred shares have the right to receive all back dividends, as well as current dividend payments, before any distributions can be made to common shareholders. All missed dividends accrue as arrearages. Virtually all preferred stock is cumulative.

Cumulative voting method   a voting method that allows the shareholder to allocate his or her aggregate votes on issues or directorships in any combination he or she chooses. (see Voting right; compare Statutory voting method)

Currency (Exchange) Risk   often simply called "currency risk," the risk of a foreign currency value declining when one is long the currency; or of a foreign currency value increasing when one is short the currency; due to any of a variety of factors such as government policy changes, inflation level changes, economic performance, etc.

Currency transaction report   a required filing with FinCEN (Financial Crimes Enforcement Network) for receipts and disbursements of more than $10,000 in cash.

Current asset   on a balance sheet, cash, accounts receivable, marketable securities, inventory or any asset that can be turned into cash, exchanged, or sold in one year or less. (compare Fixed asset)

Current coupon bond   a corporate, municipal, or federal government bond whose current yield is close to its yield-to-maturity. Because of the bond's competitive yield, it tends to be less volatile in response to market interest rate changes; as compared to a bond whose coupon rate is far away from market yields.

Current liability   on a balance sheet, a claim on a company's assets which is payable within one year - e.g., wages and salaries, taxes, accounts payable, dividends declared, and interest on debt, and the current portion due on debt principal repayment. (compare Long term liability)

Current ratio   the ratio of total current assets to total current liabilities of a company. This measures the company's liquidity.

Current yield   the return that the dividend on a stock, or the interest on a bond, provides relative to the security's current market price. The formula for computing the current yield for a stock is the annual dividend amount divided by the stock's current market price. For a bond, the current yield is the annual interest amount divided by the bond's current market price.

CUSIP number   the security industry's nine-digit identification code (Computerized Uniform Securities Identification Program - CUSIP) given to each issue and class of a security.

Custodian account   opened by only one adult (the custodian) for the benefit of one minor without any special paperwork involved, this is a fiduciary account in which the named adult makes all of the investment decisions on behalf of the minor. This account is subject to the Uniform Gifts to Minors Act (UGMA) or Uniform Transfers to Minors Act (UTMA) as adopted in each state. Such accounts are typically opened by parents for their children, for example, as an account to accumulate funds for a college education. (see Fiduciary; compare Guardian account)

Custodian bank   for investment companies, the commercial bank or trust whose primary responsibility is safeguarding the fund's assets. Custodian banks can also act as paying agents and transfer agents for investment companies.

Customer's agreement   another term for a margin agreement, this document is signed by the customer, who is pledging all of the securities in the account as collateral for the margin loan.

Cyclical stock   the common stock of companies whose market value and performance changes directly with the phases of the business cycle. Examples include companies that produce durable goods or that are involved in building homes. (compare Counter-cyclical stock)

D

Dated date   the legal issuance date of a new bond issue, this is the date from which interest begins to accrue, even if the bond is physically issued after this date.

Day order   an order to buy or sell securities without a time notation. If nothing is said on an order at the time of entry, it is assumed to be a "Day" order. If the order is not executed or canceled, a "Day" order expires at the end of the trading session during which it was placed. (compare Good til Canceled order)

Day trader   a person who performs at least 4 day trades (a "round-turn" buy and sell) in a 5 business day period. Day traders attempt to profit from rapid-fire buy-sell trading in the same stock to lock in small price differences that can arise between market makers.

Dealer   also called a principal or a market maker, this is a FINRA member firm that makes a market in an over-the-counter security; or an exchange Specialist that makes a market in an exchange listed security.

Debenture   a long-term, unsecured corporate bond backed by the full faith and credit of the issuer.

Debit balance   the loan owed to the brokerage firm by a customer who purchases securities on margin, this starts as 50% of the purchase price of a marginable stock purchased in the account, since a margin deposit of 50% is required. The interest rate charged on the loan is based on the broker loan rate (also termed the "call loan" rate) and accrues on the debit balance daily. (compare Credit balance)

Debit spread   an option spread in which the investor simultaneously buys the option with the higher premium and sells the option with the lower premium. The net difference between the higher premium paid and the lower premium received is the debit. This type of spread is profitable if the difference (the "spread") between the premiums widens. If it is a vertical (price) debit spread, this position is profitable as well, if both positions are exercised. (see Spread; compare Credit spread)

Debt limit   for municipal general obligation bonds, a statutory or constitutional limit on the dollar amount of bonds (typically expressed as a percentage of assessed value of property) that may legally be sold by the municipality.

Debt per capita ratio   a ratio used to analyze the credit of general obligation bonds, it is the ratio of Net Overall Debt to Population of the municipality.

Debt service   the annual contributions of money necessary to pay interest on the outstanding bonds; the principal on maturing serial bonds; and the required sinking fund contributions on a term bond.

Debt service coverage ratio   1) for municipal revenue bonds, a ratio used to analyze the credit of a revenue bond issue, it is the ratio of pledged revenues to debt service requirements; 2) for corporate bonds, the ratio of income prior to paying debt service to debt service requirements (both principal and interest) for that year.

Debt service reserve fund   for municipal issues, a separate account established to receive any excess monies to be used to pay for annual debt service costs, after the required annual debt service payments have been made.

Debt statement   a document that details all of a municipality's outstanding debt that is non-self supporting, thus this debt is being carried by the taxpayers. The debt statement computes Overall Net Debt of the municipality, which consists of Net Direct Debt + Overlapping Debt. (see Net direct debt, Overlapping debt)

Debt to assessed value ratio   a ratio used to analyze the credit of a general obligation bond issue, it is the ratio of Net overall debt to Assessed value of property in the municipality. (see Net overall debt)

Debt-to-assessed valuation ratio   a measure of the credit quality of a general obligation bond issue, this is the municipality's Net Overall Debt divided by the total tax valuation (assessed value) of real estate in the municipality that is the source of taxes that service the debt. (see Net overall debt)

Debt-to-population ratio   also referred to as debt per capita ratio, a measure of the credit quality of a general obligation bond issue, this is the municipality's Net Overall Debt divided by the population in the municipality that is the source of taxes that service the debt. (see Net overall debt)

Declaration date   the day on which the Board of Directors of a company announces to the public the terms and amount of any corporate distribution to shareholders such as cash or stock dividends, a rights offering, or a stock split. Under SEC rules, this date must be at least 10 business days in advance of the Record date set by the company. (compare Record date, Ex date)

Deep discount bond   a bond, originally issued at or very near par value, that is currently selling in the market at a price that is less than 80 percent of its par value. The only reason why the bond's price will have fallen so much after issuance is because either market interest rates have increased substantially; or the credit quality of the issue has deteriorated greatly.

Default risk   the same as credit risk, this is the risk that an issuer cannot pay interest and principal as due on an outstanding debt issue. (see Credit risk)

Defeasance   this is the legal "shifting" of a municipal bondholder's claim on an issuer's taxing power or revenues onto another acceptable form of collateral. The municipal issuer will buy U.S. Government securities, Agency securities, or sometimes bank certificates of deposit; escrow them with a trustee; and use the income stream from the escrowed securities to pay the debt service on the outstanding bonds. This effectively removes all bondholder claims against the revenue source backing the original issue and enables the municipality to remove the debt from its balance sheet.

The outstanding municipal bonds are now backed by the U.S. Government securities that are held in trust. If a bond issue is defeased until maturity it is said to be "escrowed to maturity" (ETM) and is known as an advance refunded issue. If a bond is defeased until its call date, it is "escrowed to call" (ETC) and is known as a pre-refunded issue. (see Advance refunding, Pre-refunding.)

Defensive securities   a company whose business is not affected by the business cycle, thus the company does not have earnings variability due to changes in the economic cycle. Defensive stocks include pharmaceuticals, and soft drink and beer manufacturers.

Deferred compensation plan   usually available to only key, upper level employees, a pension plan in which the employee arranges in a contract with the employer to defer part of his or her compensation until retirement, disability, or death. Usually there are restrictions placed in the contract - e.g., a non-compete agreement, required consulting upon retirement - which the employee must abide by in order to receive the deferred compensation.

Deficiency letter   a notice from the Securities and Exchange Commission to an issuer who has filed a registration statement under the Securities Act of 1933, that the disclosure is not adequate. The registration statement must be amended, and the 20 day cooling off period starts recounting from the date of the amendment filing. (see Cooling off period)

Defined benefit plan   a tax-qualified pension plan in which the employer promises to provide each covered person with a pre-set benefit amount upon retirement. Since this type of plan must pay the pre-set amount at retirement, larger contributions must be made on behalf of older employees that are close to retirement to fund their benefit; while much smaller contributions are required for younger employees who have a long time to retirement. The employer hires an actuary to determine the annual contribution that must be made to the plan in order to provide this benefit. The employer must contribute to this plan regardless of the profitability of the company. (compare Defined contribution plan)

Defined contribution plan   a tax-qualified pension plan to which the employer makes pre-set annual contribution amount that is computed typically as a percentage of the employee's income. Thus, the longer the employee is in the plan, the greater the pension benefit will be. An employer must contribute the pre-determined amount to the plan regardless of the company's profitability. (compare Defined benefit plan)

Deflation   a decline in the prices of goods and services, typically due to falling demand. Deflation is most likely to occur in periods of recession or depression. (see Recession, Depression; compare Inflation)

Depletion   an annual non-cash expense deducted for the "using up" of natural resources (e.g., oil, gas, timber) owned by a business. In a direct participation program (DPP), the depletion allowance enables the business to recover the cost of buying the natural resource. The depletion allowance can be computed on a cost or percentage basis. Under cost depletion, the business deducts the actual cost of purchasing the natural resource as it is used up. Under percentage depletion, the business deducts a percentage (set by Congress) of the price at which the natural resource is sold, regardless of its actual cost. (compare Depreciation)

Depreciation   1) an annual non-cash expense deducted from a business's income to reflect the "wearing out" of a fixed asset. Depreciation may be deducted on a straight-line or accelerated basis. Under straight-line depreciation, the deductions are spread evenly over the life of the asset. Under accelerated depreciation, the deductions are highest in the early years of the asset's life and lower in the later years. Methods of accelerated depreciation include double declining balance and sum of the years digits; 2) the loss in value of an asset held for investment. (compare Depletion, Appreciation)

Depression   a decline in the Gross Domestic Product (or Gross National Product) for 18 consecutive months. (compare Recession)

Derivative security   a security whose value is derived from the cash flows or price movements of an underlying instrument. Collateralized mortgage obligations and options are derivative securities.

Descending yield curve   a graph of the yields of fixed income securities of the same type (e.g., U.S. Governments or Corporates or Municipals) by maturity. As the maturity lengthens, the yield decreases, so the curve "descends." This is an unusual yield curve shape, that occurs when the Federal Reserve Board has tightened credit to slow down the economy. The Fed exerts its influence over short term rates, so its actions to tighten credit have increased short term rates above long term rates. (see Yield curve; compare Ascending yield curve, Flat yield curve, Normal yield curve)

Designated order   in the underwriting of a new issue municipal bond, an order for the new issue where the buyer designates the specific syndicate member(s) that will receive the takedown. Designated orders are filled after pre-sale and group net orders. (see Takedown, Pre-Sale order, Group Net order, Member order, Priority provisions)

Designated Order Turnaround System   the NYSE's automated trading system, known under the acronym DOT, or SuperDOT system. (see SuperDOT)

Devaluation   a reduction in the value of one country's currency in comparison to that of another country.

Developmental oil and gas program   an oil and gas partnership that drills adjacent to existing fields. These are known as "step-out" wells, since the wells drilled are "stepping-out" from the nearby field. (compare Income oil and gas program, Exploratory oil and gas program)

Diagonal spread   an option spread position, where simultaneously the same type of option is bought and sold with different strike prices; and different expirations. When the positions are "stacked" one above the other, there is a vertical difference in the strike prices, and a horizontal difference in the expirations. Combine a vertical with a horizontal, and the result is a "diagonal" spread. (compare Vertical spread, Horizontal spread)

DIAMOND   commonly used name for the Dow Jones Industrial Average Exchange Traded Fund, an index fund traded on the American Stock Exchange under the symbol DIA.

Dilution   a term applied to earnings per share (EPS) indicating an increase in the number of outstanding common shares which results in a company's earnings being spread over more shares; hence, its EPS decreases. Dilution is caused by stock dividends and stock splits, conversion of convertible bonds and preferred stock, exercise of rights and warrants, and exercise of stock options granted to company officers and employees. (see Earnings per share)

Direct debt   debt that a municipality has issued solely in its own name.

Direct participation program (DPP)   more commonly known as a limited partnership or tax shelter, this is a partnership that permits the gains and losses of the business to flow through from the program to the investors (known as limited partners) without the partnership having any tax liability. The partners include the items of income and loss on their individual tax returns, and hence directly participate in the results of the enterprise. (see Limited partnerships, Tax shelters)

Direct plus   the newest electronic order matching system used by the NYSE, Direct + bypasses Specialists and Floor Brokers for extremely fast executions. In comparison, the NYSE SuperDOT system allows for human interaction to "improve" the price of orders sent to the trading floor, but this slows down the time needed to fill an order

Direct registration system   abbreviated DRS, this is the "book entry" registration system for stock issues, replacing printed stock certificates.

Discount   1) the amount by which the market value of a bond or preferred stock is below its par value; 2) the amount below par value paid for a security. (compare Premium)

Discount bond   a bond currently selling below par value. Stated another way, the amount by which the par value of a bond exceeds the market value. (compare Premium bond)

Discount rate the interest rate which the Federal Reserve charges member banks for making direct loans of reserves. This rate is typically set at 100 basis points (1%) higher than the Fed Funds rate. Making changes to the discount rate is a monetary policy tool employed by the Fed to tighten or loosen the money supply. (compare Federal funds rate)

Discretionary account requiring a written power of attorney, an account in which an investor gives the broker authority to choose the amount and/or the security to be traded in the account. Note that no power of attorney is needed for a broker to select the price and time of execution in an account - this is not considered to be "discretionary."

Discretionary order an order where the registered representative selects the security and the number of shares for a customer. Discretionary orders must be marked as such, require that a power of attorney from the customer be on file, and require extra supervisory review. Note that no power of attorney is needed for a broker to select the price and time of execution in a trade - this is not considered to be "discretionary." (see Discretionary account)

Disintermediation the flow of funds from the holdings of financial intermediaries (such as banks and savings and loans) into direct investments in securities. Disintermediation occurs when the interest rate offered by banks to depositors is substantially lower than the interest rates available in the market for very safe investments, such as Treasury Bills. (compare Intermediation)

Disproportionate sharing arrangement in an oil and gas program, an arrangement where the general partner agrees to bear a percentage of the costs for a much larger percentage of the oil revenue. (compare Overriding royalty interest, Net profits interest, Reversionary working interest))

District Hearing Panel formerly known as the "DBCC" - District Business Conduct Committee, a panel formed in each of FINRA/NASD's 11 districts to hear customer complaints, and take sanctions against member firms for violations.

Diversification   investing in a variety of securities to reduce risk. Diversification of stocks is accomplished by investing in companies in different lines of business; and in different geographic areas. Diversification of fixed income investments is accomplished by investing securities of different issuers, with different credit ratings, with different maturities, and in issuers in different geographic areas.

Diversified fund   a definition under the Investment Company Act of 1940, a diversified fund is one that meets the "75/5/10" rule. To be diversified, a fund must have at least 75% of its assets invested in securities; with no more than 5% of these assets invested in any one company's securities; with no holding exceeding 10% of the voting stock of any one company. (compare Non-diversified fund)

Divestiture   when a company has a line of business or a subsidiary that no longer fits into its long range business plans, it may "divest" itself of this business by selling it to an interested buyer.

Divided syndicate   the same as a Western syndicate account, a syndicate agreement in which each member is only responsible and liable for selling the fixed amount of the issue it is allocated. Each member's liability is unaffected by the performance of the other syndicate members. (compare Eastern syndicate, Undivided account)

Dividend   that portion of the company's earnings per share which its Board of Directors decides to distribute to the shareholders. Cash dividends paid to common shareholders are usually distributed quarterly, whereas preferred dividends are typically paid semi-annually. Additionally, a company can pay dividends in stock, when it wishes to conserve cash; and it believes that the additional shares will not dilute future earnings because it is growing rapidly.

Dividend pay out ratio   the percentage of a company's total earnings for common shareholders that were actually distributed as dividends to the common shareholders.

Dividend reinvestment plan   also known as a "DRIP" - (Dividend ReInvestment Plan), a plan whereby a company's existing shareholders choose to have their cash dividend payments automatically reinvested in additional shares of the company's stock. Since the new shares are directly sold by the company to existing shareholders, there are no brokerage commissions to be paid by the customer.

DJX   abbreviation for the Dow Jones Industrial Average Index option contract, traded on the CBOE. Unlike other index options, which have a strike price equal to the index value, the DJX has a strike price equal to 1/100th of the index value.

DK   slang abbreviation of Don't Know, a notice sent from one broker-dealer to a contra broker-dealer when the trade data submitted on the comparison cannot be reconciled. DKs are also called questionable trades (QTs) at the New York Stock Exchange. (see Comparison)

DNR   abbreviation for Do Not Reduce. This is placed on an order that is below the market if a customer does not want the order price automatically reduced on ex date. (see Ex date)

Do not reduce   a notation placed on a contingency orders place below the prevailing market that instructs the Specialist not to reduce the price specified on the order on a stock's ex date. (see Ex date)

Dollar bond   1) industry slang for a municipal bond that is quoted in terms of its dollar price instead of its yield to maturity. Municipal term bonds are generally dollar bonds; whereas municipal serial bonds are generally quoted on a yield basis; 2) bonds issued outside the U.S. that are denominated in dollars, for example, Eurodollar bonds.

Dollar-cost averaging   a strategy whereby a person invests the same amount of money at regular intervals in a stock or a mutual fund without regard for the price fluctuations of the security. Over time, this investment strategy usually results in an investor's average cost per share for the security being lower than the security's average price per share over the same period.

Don't know notice abbreviated as a "DK," a notice sent from one broker-dealer to a contra broker-dealer when the trade data submitted on the comparison cannot be reconciled. DKs are also called questionable trades (QTs) at the New York Stock Exchange. (see Comparison)

DOT the NYSE's automated trading system, known under the acronym DOT - Designated Order Turnaround system, or SuperDOT system (see SuperDOT)

Double declining balance an accelerated depreciation method available for tangible assets such as equipment that, in essence, "doubles up" on the depreciation amounts allowed in the early years of an asset's life; with the deductions reduced proportionately in the later years; as compared to straight line depreciation. (see Accelerated depreciation)

Double-barreled bond a municipal revenue bond whose principal and interest payments are backed by ad valorem taxing power in addition to the revenue pledge.

Dow Jones Averages the oldest measure of the activity and movement of the overall market, which consists of 30 industrial stocks, 20 transportation stocks and 15 utility stocks. Thus, there is a total of 65 stocks in the Dow Jones Averages. Note that the average for the 30 industrial stocks, called the Dow Jones Industrial Average (DJIA), is the most widely quoted, and narrowest measure, of stock market movement.

Dow Jones Industrial Average the most widely quoted index, consisting of 30 companies (mainly NYSE listed issues), selected to mirror the make-up of the largest sectors of the United States economy.

Dow Jones Industrial Average Index option abbreviated DJX, the Dow Jones Industrial Average Index option contract is traded on the CBOE. Unlike other index options, which have a strike price equal to the index value, the DJX has a strike price equal to 1/100th of the index value.

Dow theory   a rather archaic technical theory that states that any uptrend in the Dow Jones Industrial Average must be confirmed by an uptrend in the Dow Jones Transportations Average for that market trend to be valid. Conversely, any downtrend in the Dow Jones Industrial Average must be confirmed by a downtrend in the Dow Jones Transportations Average for that market trend to be valid. The idea is that the production of the goods shows in the industrial stocks as sales and earnings improvement, driving the industrial average upward as investors respond to the good news; but if the additional production is not being moved to market (as shown by improved sales and earnings in the transportation stocks) then no one wants to buy those goods, and the upward movement cannot be sustained. (see Dow Jones averages)

Downtrend   the downward movement of a stock's price, or the market as whole as measured by an average or index, over a period of time. (compare Uptrend)

Dual agency transaction   a trade in which the customer sells a security and uses the proceeds to buy another security. The two parts of this transaction are subject to two separate commissions in agency transactions. Under FINRA/NASD rules, the separate commissions are combined and the total charge is less than if two totally separate transactions had been performed. This is also known as a "proceeds" transaction.

Dual purpose fund   an investment company that issues 2 classes of shares from the same portfolio - growth shares and income shares. Once the investor selects the class of shares to invest in, he or she owns essentially either a growth fund; or an income fund. These are virtually obsolete.

Dual listed   a security that is traded in more than one marketplace - for example, a young West Coast company might have listed on the Pacific exchange when it was still small; and then listed on the NYSE when the company became large enough. Also note that the major exchanges (NYSE, AMEX, NASDAQ) had rules discouraging "dual listing" with each other, but the SEC views this as "anti-competitive" and these rules have been rescinded.

Due bill   a notice sent from a broker-dealer to the contra broker-dealer on settlement indicating that the buying customer is rightfully due the dividend that has been sent by the issuer, in error, to the seller of the stock. The seller must remit a "due bill check" in the amount of the dividend to the buyer. Due bills are required when a customer buys before ex date, however settlement is delayed, usually due to some problem, until after Record date. Due bills are also used where the amount of accrued interest on a bond trade has been computed improperly. (see Ex date, Record date)

Due bill check   a post-dated check, dated on the Payable date for a cash dividend on stock, which is owed to a buying customer who submitted a due bill. The due bill is a notice sent from a broker-dealer to the contra broker-dealer on settlement indicating that the buying customer is rightfully due the dividend that has been sent by the issuer, in error, to the seller of the stock. The seller must remit a "due bill check" in the amount of the dividend to the buyer. Due bills are required when a customer buys before ex date, however settlement is delayed, usually due to some problem, until after Record date. (see Ex date, Payable date, Record date)

Due diligence   under the Securities Act of 1933, any omissions or misstatements of material fact in a registration statement or prospectus are fraud for all persons who have signed the registration statement. Thus, these persons must perform "due diligence" to insure that there is full disclosure to investors. The signers include the officers of the issuer; the accountants and lawyers involved in preparing the documents; and the underwriter.

Dutch auction   a rarely used auction technique for securities, where competitive interest rate bids are progressively accepted from lowest to highest until the entire issue is placed (similar to the Treasury auction). However, in a Dutch auction, all of the securities get the same interest rate - and that rate is the last one (highest one) accepted. This eliminates what is known as the "winner's curse" in a competitive bid auction - that is bidding an interest rate that is lower than that of another winning bidder.

Durable power of attorney   a power of attorney that continues in force upon the mental incapacitation of the grantor (compare non-durable power of attorney).

E

Earned income   a definition under the tax code, this is wages and salaries earned in an occupation, net of the expenses necessary to earn that income. (compare Portfolio income, Passive income)

Earned surplus   another name for retained earnings, these are earnings of the company that have not been paid to shareholders as a dividend. They have been retained for use in the business.

Earnings for common   by deducting the preferred dividend from a corporation's net income after tax, leaves earnings for common. This is the earnings figure that is used to compute Earnings per share (EPS).

Earnings per share (EPS)   that portion of a company's profit that is allocated to each outstanding common share after bond interest, taxes, and preferred dividends have been paid. A company's Board of Directors decides what portion of the EPS is distributed as a dividend to common shareholders.

Eastern syndicate   a syndicate agreement in which each member has technically unlimited selling responsibility and unlimited liability. Typical for municipal underwritings, each member takes a percentage of the offering. This percentage does not limit sales by the member. However, if securities remain unsold out of the total syndicate account, each member is liable for that percentage of all unsold securities. Thus, each member's liability is affected by the performance of all other syndicate members. (compare Western syndicate)

ECN   abbreviation for an Electronic Communications Network, these are electronic order books of customer buy and sell orders that are matched for execution by such firms as Instinet, Island (now a wholly owned subsidiary of Instinet) and Archipelago (now owned by the NYSE) in the Fourth Market. (see Fourth market)

ECU   a commonly used term and acronym for European Currency Unit, a weighted basket of the currencies of the countries that make up the European Economic Community

Education IRA   a type of tax deferred account that allows a maximum aggregate $2000 non-deductible contribution to be made for the purpose of paying for a child's higher education expenses. (compare IRA, Roth IRA)

Effective date   the first date that a new issue can be sold to the public under the provisions of the Securities Act of 1933. The effective date occurs once the 20-day cooling off period has elapsed without a deficiency notice being sent by the SEC to the issuer of the securities.

Efficient market   a trading market that is characterized by high trading volumes, which minimize marketability risk, and narrow dealer spreads. Such markets have lower transaction costs for investors to buy and sell, minimizing liquidity risk as well. (see Spread, Marketability risk, Liquidity risk; compare Thin market)

Efficient market theory   the theory that all information about an issuer is available to all participants in the market at the same time and that the prices of securities directly reflect investor expectations based on this information. Therefore, attempting to profit from buying undervalued stocks or selling short overvalued stocks is futile. Most accepted is the "semi-strong" version of this theory, which states that market valuations reflect all "publicly known" information about an issuer; but do not reflect information known only by "insiders" - the officers and directors of that company.

Either/Or   a notation placed on two contingency orders instructing the floor broker to execute one or the other. An example is an order to "Buy 1000 ABC at $40; or Sell 1000 ABC at $60." If one of the orders is filled in part or in full, then an equal amount of the other order is canceled.

Electronic Bulletin Board   FINRA's electronic version of the "Pink Sheets," the OTCBB (Over-The-Counter Bulletin Board) displays dealer quotes for OTC issues that are too small to be included in NASDAQ (compare Pink Sheets; see OTC Bulletin Board)

Eligible security   a security that is acceptable for trading with the Federal Reserve in its open market operations. U.S. Government securities, Agency securities, and prime banker's acceptances are eligible securities. (see Open market operations)

EPS   the acronym for Earnings per Share, this is Net Income After Tax, reduced by any preferred dividends paid; divided by the number of common shares outstanding.

Equipment trust certificate   a long-term debt security issued by corporations that are common carriers such as airlines and railroads. The proceeds from the issue are used to purchase equipment such as aircraft or railroad cars, to which a trustee holds the title for the certificate holders until the bond is retired. If there is a default or bankruptcy, the certificate holders have first claim on the equipment pledged as collateral for the loan.

Equity   a person's ownership interest in a securities account. The entire market value is the equity in a cash account; the excess of long market value over the debit balance is the equity in a long margin account; the excess of credit balance over the short market value is the equity in a short margin account. (see Debit Balance; Credit balance)

Equity fund   a mutual fund that invests only in common and/or preferred stocks.

Equity REIT   a Real Estate Investment Trust that buys or leases real estate. Shareholders' dividends are paid from the lease or rental income from the property. Shareholders also receive capital gains when the property the REIT owns is sold. (compare Mortgage REIT)

Equity security   commonly called a stock or a share, a security representing a proportionate ownership of a business and the right to receive dividends. Common and preferred stock are equity securities.

ERISA   acronym for Employee Retirement Income Security Act, the 1974 act which regulates for-profit employer-sponsored pension plans. A plan that meets ERISA's guidelines for vesting, non-discrimination, and fiduciary responsibility is considered a tax-qualified plan. (see Tax-qualified plan, Vesting)

Escrowed to maturity   a municipal bond issue where the bondholder's claim on an issuer's taxing power or revenues has been shifted onto another acceptable form of collateral. The municipal issuer will buy U.S. Government securities, Agency securities, or sometimes bank certificates of deposit; escrow them with a trustee; and use the income stream from the escrowed securities to pay the debt service on the outstanding bonds.

This effectively removes all bondholder claims against the revenue source backing the original issue and enables the municipality to remove the debt from its balance sheet. The outstanding municipal bonds are now backed by the U.S. Government securities that are held in trust. If a bond issue is defeased until maturity it is said to be "escrowed to maturity" (ETM) and is known as an advance refunded issue.

Estate account   a type of fiduciary account of a person since deceased, managed by the executor of the estate.

Euro   the common currency of countries that have joined the European Monetary Union (EMU). There are 12 countries in the "Euro" zone, with the largest participants being Germany, France and Italy. Note that Great Britain and Switzerland have not yet joined the EMU.

Eurodollar U.S. dollars held in banks in European countries. Originally, these dollars were used to facilitate international trade payments. Today, many European countries issue Eurodollar securities. The dividend or interest payment on these securities will be made using the U.S. dollars on deposit in the European banks.

Eurodollar bonds bonds issued outside the United States whose principal and interest will be paid in dollars. The bonds can be issued by an American or European corporations, and by sovereign governments and municipal governments. (see Eurodollar)

European currency unit abbreviated as ECU, a weighted basket of the currencies of the countries that make up the European Economic Community (EEC).

European style option a call or put option that can be exercised only at expiration. (compare American style option)

Exchange Traded Funds index funds such as Spiders (Standard and Poor's 500 Index Fund shares); Diamonds (Dow Jones Industrial Average Index Fund Shares); and Qubes (NASDAQ 100 Index Fund Shares). Exchange traded index funds, as compared to index mutual funds, are traded throughout the day and can be purchased on margin.

Ex date the day on which the price of the stock is reduced by the dividend amount and anyone purchasing the stock will no longer be eligible to receive the dividend. The NYSE and NASDAQ set the ex dividend date for cash dividends at 2 business days prior to the Record date (since regular way settlement takes 3 business days, anyone who buys 3 business days or more prior to the Record date will settle on, or before, the Record date and will receive the dividend). The ex date for non-cash distributions such as stock splits, stock dividends, and rights is set at the business day following the Payable date. (see Payable date)

Ex rights literally "without" rights, this term describes the date from which transactions in the common stock are no longer accompanied by subscription rights. On the ex date, the price of the stock is reduced for the value of the rights that no longer accompany the stock. The rights, at this time, trade separately in the market, until their expiration. (see Subscription right; compare Cum-rights)

Ex rights / Ex stock dividend date   different than the ex date for cash dividends, the ex date for non-cash distributions is set at the business day after the payable date. Due to this unusual ex date, between the record date and the payable date, the securities will trade with a due bill for the extra shares or rights issued as a result of the distribution. (see Due bill)

Exchange rate   also called the foreign exchange rate, the price at which one country's currency can be converted into another country's currency. Most exchange rates are described as "floating" because they change daily in response to supply and demand forces in the market place, as determined by trading in the interbank market. Other exchange rates are "fixed," set by a country's government or central bank (usually for those countries that are less developed). (see Interbank market)

Exchange rate risk   the risk of a foreign currency value declining when one is long the currency; or of a foreign currency value increasing when one is short the currency; due to any of a variety of factors such as government policy changes, inflation level changes, economic performance, etc.

Exempt security   securities, including governmental issues such as U.S. Government securities, Agency securities, municipal bonds; money market instruments such as commercial paper and banker's acceptances; and issuers that are regulated under other laws such as banks, insurance companies and common carriers; that are exempt from the provisions of the Securities Act of 1933 and the Securities and Exchange Act of 1934 (except for the anti-fraud provisions).

Exempt transactions   defined under the Securities Act of 1933, these are unregistered securities offerings that are exempt from registration. Exempt transactions include private placements under Regulation D; intrastate offerings under Rule 147; small dollar offerings under Regulation A; and Rule 144 transactions.

Exercise   1) converting a convertible security into common stock; 2) buying the common stock of an issuer by converting a right or warrant; 3) buying the common shares (or other underlying instrument) at a fixed price stated in a call option contract; 4) selling the common shares (or other underlying instrument) at a fixed price stated in a put option contract.

Exercise limit   a limitation on the number of option contracts that can be exercised during a 5 business day time period, established by the Options Clearing Corporation.

Expected rate of return   the rate of return that an investment is "expected" to return. It is computed by assigning probabilities to various scenarios for that investment's potential returns.

Expense guarantee   a guarantee that the expenses charged to the purchaser of an annuity contract will not rise above a certain level. If they do, then the insurance company agrees to absorb the excess. (compare Mortality guarantee)

Expense ratio   a measure of efficiency for a mutual fund, this ratio shows the portion of a fund's return on net assets that is "eaten up" by the expenses of running the fund. The expense ratio is the ratio of total expenses to total net assets.

Expiration date   the day of the month in which an option contract expires, established by the Options Clearing Corporation. Equity and index options expire on the Saturday following the third Friday of the month. Foreign currency options expire on the Saturday preceding the third Wednesday of the month.

Exploratory oil and gas program   a limited partnership that drills for oil and gas far away from existing fields. These are known as "wildcat" wells. (compare Income oil and gas program, Developmental oil and gas program)

Extension risk   the risk associated with mortgage backed pass-through certificates and their derivatives such as CMOs - collateralized mortgage obligations, that interest rates will rise substantially after issuance, inducing homeowners to stay in their existing homes. Thus, expected prepayment rates fall, and the life of the certificates goes much longer than expected, during which period the certificate holder earns a lower than market rate of return. (see CMO, Mortgage backed security, Pass-through security; compare Prepayment risk)

Extraordinary item   found on a company's income statement, this is a one-time event that either substantially increases or reduces the company's reported income for that year. Since it did not occur as a result of the company's regular operations, it is segregated and shown separately on the income statement. Examples of extraordinary items would be charges taken to shut down a plant; accounting gains occurring from a merger, etc.

Extraordinary mandatory call   a call provision in a bond contract that specifies extraordinary circumstances when the issuer must call in the bonds, such as a calamity call. (see Calamity call)

Extraordinary optional call   a call covenant that gives the issuer the option of calling in bonds if an extraordinary event occurs. An example is a call covenant on a housing bond issue that allows the issuer to call in bonds if the mortgages are paid off earlier than expected. Note, however, that the issuer is not required to call in the bonds.

_F_

Face amount certificate   one of the three types of investment companies defined in the Investment Company Act of 1940. The purchaser of this instrument agrees to pay a fixed amount either periodically or in a lump sum. In return, the issuer agrees to pay the purchaser the face amount of the certificate at some future date. The face amount is always greater than the investor's total periodic payments - the difference being the income earned on the certificate. Few of these certificates are issued today.

Fail to deliver   when a security is sold, but the seller fails to deliver the security to the buyer on settlement date. Under the 1934 Act, customer fails to deliver must be closed-out (bought-in) by the brokerage firm no later than 10 business days after settlement. (compare Fail to receive)

Fail to receive   when a security is purchased, and then the buyer does not receive the security on settlement date. (compare Fail to deliver)

Family of funds   a group of different funds with different investment objectives, all sponsored by the same fund company. For example, all Dreyfus funds comprise the Dreyfus fund "family."

Fannie Mae   the commonly used name for the Federal National Mortgage Association - FNMA, a privatized agency that makes a secondary market in mortgages. FNMA is a listed company whose stock trades on the New York Stock Exchange.

FDIC   the Federal Deposit Insurance Corporation, which insures customer bank accounts against bank failure. (compare SIPC)

Feasibility study   conducted by independent consultants, a study performed to determine if a proposed municipal revenue bond will be self-supporting.

Fed funds jargon for Federal Funds, overnight loans of reserves from one Federal Reserve member bank to another Federal Reserve member bank. Loans of Fed Funds are made at the Federal Funds rate. (see Federal funds rate)

Federal Farm Credit Consolidated System established in 1971, a group of federal agencies that provide low interest rate financing to farmers. Agencies included in the consolidated system are the Federal Land Banks, Federal Intermediate Credit Banks, and Banks for Cooperatives. This agency issues bonds to finance its activities.

Federal funds 1) an overnight, unsecured loan between bank members of the Federal Reserve System, this is the shortest term money market instrument. The loan is made from a Federal Reserve member bank that has excess reserves to a member bank that is deficient in reserves; 2) monies payable the same day at a member bank of the Federal Reserve System. Trades of U.S. Government and Agency securities settle next business day in Federal funds (compare Clearing house funds).

Federal funds rate the interest rate charged on borrowings between Federal Reserve System member banks for overnight loans of reserves. Because this rate changes daily in response to the need for borrowing, it is considered an indicator of future interest rate changes. Also note that this is the lowest interest rate in the economy (see Federal funds, compare Discount rate).

Federal Home Loan Bank (FHLB) this federal agency makes loans to savings and loan (S&L) institutions, where the mortgages made by the S&Ls are the collateral for the loan. In essence, the FHLB makes a secondary market in mortgages. To finance its activities, the FHLB issues non-callable, book-entry bonds, and short-term discount notes.

Federal Home Loan Mortgage Corporation commonly called "Freddie Mac," this federal agency buys conventional single-family residential mortgages from lenders, pools them, and sells pass-through certificates to investors that represent an undivided interest in the pool. Payments from Freddie Macs consist of both interest and principal (the same as the underlying mortgage payments), the interest portion of which is fully taxable; hence FHLMC bonds are referred to as participation certificates. Freddie Mac is a "privatized" federal agency that is now a for-profit company whose common stock is listed on the NYSE. (see Participation certificates)

Federal Intermediate Credit Banks part of the Federal Farm Credit Consolidated System, this agency provides short term, seasonal loans to farmers that are primarily used for agricultural production. This agency funds its activities by issuing short-term notes and debentures. (see Federal Farm Credit Consolidated System)

Federal Land Banks part of the Federal Farm Credit Consolidated System, this agency provides long-term loans to farmers, using the farmers' real estate (i.e., land and farm buildings) as collateral. This agency issues conventional bonds to finance its activities. (see Federal Farm Credit Consolidated System)

Federal National Mortgage Association (FNMA) the full name for the U.S. Government agency that issues bonds and pass-through certificates most commonly referred to as Fannie Maes. FNMA buys federally-insured and conventional mortgages from lenders, thereby providing the lenders with more money to make mortgage loans. FNMA then repackages the mortgages it buys into the pools and issues mortgage backed pass-through certificates. Payments from FNMA certificates are "pass throughs" of monthly mortgage payments, and therefore include both interest and principal, of which the interest portion is fully taxable. FNMA is a "privatized" federal agency that is now a for-profit company whose common stock is listed on the NYSE.

Federal Open Market Committee   comprised of the presidents of six Federal Reserve Banks and seven governors of the Federal Reserve, the FOMC meets about every 6 weeks and decides what monetary policy actions should be taken (if any). If the FOMC decides that credit needs to be loosened, it will direct the Federal Reserve trading desk in New York to buy U.S. Government and eligible securities from Fed member banks, thereby injecting the banks with funds. If the FOMC decides that credit needs to be tightened, it will direct the Federal Reserve trading desk in New York to sell U.S. Government and eligible securities to Fed member banks, thereby draining the banks of funds.

Federal Reserve Board (FRB)   the governing board of the Federal Reserve system which sets the policies that affect the money supply. The "Fed" oversees the activities of the 12 regional Federal Reserve Banks. Tools of the Fed include changing reserve requirements, changing the discount rate, conducting open market operations, and changing margin requirements on non-exempt securities under Regulation T.

Federal Telephone Consumer Protection Act   federal legislation enacted in 1991 that sets requirements for commercial "cold calls" over the telephone. The Act limits the times that calls can be made; requires identification of the caller; and requires that "Do Not Call" lists be maintained if the customer does not wish to be called.

FGIC   acronym for Financial Guaranty Insurance Corporation, a private company to which a municipality pays a fee to insure the timely payment of interest and principal on a bond issue. This "insurance" results in a better credit rating and lower interest cost to the issuer. (see AMBAC, MBIA, BIGI)

Fidelity bond   also called a blanket fidelity bond, insurance coverage which a firm must have to protect itself if securities are lost or stolen by employees.

Fiduciary account   a company, trust or person who holds or invests funds for someone else, acting in the best interest of the account owner. Trust, guardian, and custodian accounts are all fiduciary accounts.

FIFO   1) the abbreviation for first in, first out, this is an accounting method in which inventory is assumed to be sold in the order in which it was received; 2) for contingency orders on the Specialist's book, the execution of all orders at the same price in the order in which they were received; 3) for tax accounting, the first transaction to occur results in the first tax event when the securities giving rise to the transaction are sold or payments are taken that result from that transaction. (compare LIFO)

Fill or kill   abbreviated FOK on an order ticket, a notation on a contingency order instructing the floor broker to attempt to execute the entire order at one price in one try. If the order cannot be executed in full the first time, it is canceled. (compare All or none, Immediate or cancel)

Financial advisor   in a municipal bond underwriting, the individual or company that advises the municipality about the structuring and marketing of a new issue, including its backing, maturity, and likely coupon rate.

Financial and Operations Principal   a license designation for an individual who has passed the Series #27 examination. This person is qualified to prepare the member firm's accounting reports that must be filed the SEC and the exchange.

Financial profile   an assessment of an investor's assets, liabilities, investment objectives, and willingness to assume risk.

Financial statements   the generic name for the balance sheet, income statement, statement of changes to retained earnings, and flow of funds statement that a company must file with the SEC and send to investors regularly. (see Balance sheet, Income statement)

FINRA   acronym for the Financial Industry Regulatory Authority, the new regulator for member firms created in mid-2007 from the merger of the NYSE and NASD regulatory groups. FINRA intends to create a new uniform body of rules for the industry, since NYSE and NASD rules often do not match, resulting in excessive compliance costs.

Firm commitment underwriting a type of underwriting commitment in which the underwriter, acting as a principal, agrees to buy all of an issuer's new securities and then resell sell them to the public. The issuer is, therefore, guaranteed its funds and the underwriter assumes full financial liability if the security cannot be sold to the public. (compare Best efforts commitment)

Firm offer with a recall in municipal trading, a selling dealer will offer bonds at a firm price to a buying dealer for a limited period of time (say 1/2 hour). This gives the buying dealer the ability to "shop around," confident in the knowledge that he can always get the bonds at the firm offer price. However, the selling dealer may specify a "recall" (say a 5 minute recall). This gives the selling dealer the right to contact the buying dealer any time during the 1/2 hour to demand that a purchase decision be made within the next 5 minutes. The right of recall would be exercised by the selling dealer if another customer came along during the 1/2 hour who wanted to buy those exact bonds.

Firm quote in the over-the-counter market, the price quote at which a dealer will trade a round lot of a security. This is a "firm" price - the dealer cannot change the price once the quote is given. Failure to honor a firm quote, known as "backing away," is prohibited. All NASDAQ quotes are "firm." (compare Nominal quote, Subject quote)

First market the trading market (secondary market) is subcategorized into the First, Second, Third, and Fourth markets. The First market is trading of exchange listed securities on the exchange floor. It is called the "first market" because trading on an exchange floor was the very first securities market in the United States; for example the NYSE started trading in 1794. (compare Second market, Third market, Fourth market)

First mortgage bond a secured corporate bond that is backed by a first mortgage on real property. This is also called a senior lien bond; because there can be Second mortgage bonds issued ("junior lien bonds") that have a lower claim priority on the property. Mortgage bonds are typically issued by utilities. (compare Second mortgage bond)

First party   regarding brokerage accounts, the parties to the account are: First Party - Brokerage Firm; Second Party - Customer; Third Party - Anyone other than the Brokerage Firm or Customer.

Fiscal policy   actions taken by the federal government, and approved by Congress, to increase business activity and the growth of the economy. These actions include changing federal income tax rates, changing transfer payments (Social Security), and changing the way the government spends money for goods and services. (compare Monetary policy)

Fitch's Investors Services   a ratings service that rates bonds for credit risk, Fitch's is the smallest of the "big 3" credit ratings services. In the year 2000, Fitch's bought the smallest of the ratings services, Duff and Phelps, with the new company still being called Fitch's. The credit ratings services are (from biggest to smallest) Moody's; Standard and Poor's; and Fitch's.

Fixed annuity   an annuity that pays the annuitant a fixed amount for life, or for a fixed period of time. Because the insurance company issuing the contract bears all of the investment risk, in most states a fixed annuity is an insurance product, not a security. (see Annuity; compare Variable annuity)

Fixed asset   on a balance sheet, tangible assets such as property, plant, and equipment that are carried on the balance sheet at their net depreciated value. (compare Current asset)

Fixed UIT   a type of Unit Investment Trust under the Investment Company Act of 1940, in which a portfolio, usually containing one type of security (bonds), is set up and does not change - so the portfolio composition is fixed (hence the name). Units of the portfolio are sold to the public. Interest from the bonds held in the portfolio is distributed to the unit holders periodically. As the securities mature, or are called, the portfolio self-liquidates.

Flat bond   a bond trading without accrued interest. Bonds that are in default, income (a.k.a. adjustment) bonds, and zero-coupon bonds trade flat.

Flat yield curve   a graph of the yields of fixed income securities of the same type (e.g., U.S. Governments or Corporates or Municipals) by maturity. As the maturity lengthens, the yields are about the same, so the curve is "flat." This is an unusual yield curve shape, that occurs when the economy is in transition from an "easy money" phase to a "tight money" phase. The Fed exerts its influence over short term rates (which normally are lower than long term rates). If the Fed takes actions to tighten credit, then short term rates will increase. If short term rates increase to about the same level as long term rates, then the yield curve moves from an "ascending" curve to a "flat" curve. If the Fed tightens further, then the curve can "invert" - with short term rates driven higher than long term rates. (see Yield curve; compare Ascending yield curve, Descending yield curve, Normal yield curve)

Floaters   a commonly used name for securities with floating (variable) interest rates.

Floating rate note   a debt security with a typical maturity of five to seven years whose interest rate is periodically adjusted, annually or semi-annually. The new interest rate is tied to some predetermined rate, such as the 6-month Treasury Bill rate.

Floating rate preferred stock   another name for adjustable rate preferred stock, where the dividend rate is adjusted to some market interest rate index, typically annually.

Floor Broker   also called a commission house broker, an employee of an exchange member firm who executes orders for the company's public customers on the exchange floor. On the NYSE, where most orders now go through SuperDOT, the exchange's automated trading system, floor brokers handle orders that are too large for SuperDOT; or "special instruction" orders that cannot be entered into the automated system, such as Market-Not Held orders. Floor brokers act solely as agents on the stock exchange floor. (compare Specialist, Competitive trader)

Floor Governor   a person who oversees trading activities on an exchange floor.

Floor Trader   a registered exchange member, only on the CBOE floor, who trades for his or her own account, at his or her own risk. (see Competitive trader, Floor broker)

Flow of funds   the order in which income from a facility backing a revenue bond is to be collected and disbursed to pay the expenses of the facility and the debt service on the outstanding bonds. The "flow of funds" is stated in the bond contract and trust indenture (see Net revenue pledge, Gross revenue pledge)

Flow of funds indicators   statistics that enable an analyst to determine in which markets - money market, stock market, bond market, savings accounts, etc. - individuals and institutions will most likely invest their money during given economic conditions or periods of time. (see Disintermediation, Intermediation)

FOK   abbreviation for a Fill or Kill order, this order type is to be filled in its entirety or canceled. (compare AON, IOC)

FOMC   comprised of the presidents of six Federal Reserve Banks and seven governors of the Federal Reserve, the FOMC meets about every 6 weeks and decides what monetary policy actions should be taken (if any). If the FOMC decides that credit needs to be loosened, it will direct the Federal Reserve trading desk in New York to buy U.S. Government and eligible securities from Fed member banks, thereby injecting the banks with funds. If the FOMC decides that credit needs to be tightened, it will direct the Federal Reserve trading desk in New York to sell U.S. Government and eligible securities to Fed member banks, thereby draining the banks of funds.

Forced conversion   when an issuer calls in convertible preferred stock or convertible bonds that are trading in the market at a substantial premium. Rather than accept the low "call" price, the holder of these securities will convert into common shares. Thus, the issuer is "forcing conversion" of the issue. After conversion, there will be more common shares outstanding, and fewer convertible senior securities outstanding.

Foreign currency contract a contract traded in the "interbank market" to buy or sell a foreign currency. This is an institutional market, dominated by the money center banks, trading very large amounts of currencies. Trades of foreign currencies settle either "spot" or "forward." (see Forward settlement; Spot settlement)

Foreign currency option an option contract to either buy or sell foreign currencies at a fixed dollar (U.S.) price. Foreign currency options are traded on the Philadelphia Stock Exchange only.

Foreign currency risk also called currency exchange risk, the risk that value of an asset denominated in a foreign currency declines. This decline can occur either because the value of the foreign currency falls; or the value of the U.S. dollar rises.

Form 10K the detailed annual report that all companies who have issued securities must file with the SEC. The information contained in the reports is made public so that investors can use it to evaluate their investment. The financial statements included with this form must be audited. (see Annual report)

Form 10Q the form on which a publicly-held company must file its quarterly report with the SEC. The financial statements included in a 10Q do not have to be audited, whereas the annual 10K filing made by the issuer with the SEC must be audited.

Form 144 the public notice, filed with the SEC when the holder of restricted or control stock wishes to sell. 4 sales per year are permitted, with the maximum sale each time being the greater of 1% of the outstanding shares of the issuer; or the weekly average of the prior 4 weeks' trading volume. (see Restricted stock, Control stock)

Form 8K the SEC-required form on which a company must report any material events that might affect its financial condition or the market value of its shares. Material events requiring the issuer to file Form 8K include mergers, acquisitions, changes in the composition of the Board of Directors, and bankruptcy filings.

Forward contract   a contract to buy or sell foreign currencies in which the price and quantity are established at the time the contract is initiated, but actual delivery occurs at a predetermined date in the future. The terms of a forward contract are always negotiated between the buyer and the seller. Forward contracts trade in the "interbank" market. (see Interbank market)

Forward settlement   a contract to buy or sell foreign currencies in which the price and quantity are established at the time the contract is initiated, but actual delivery occurs at a predetermined date in the future. The terms of a forward contract are always negotiated between the buyer and the seller. Forward contracts trade in the "interbank" market. (see Interbank market; compare Spot settlement)

Fourth market   the trading market (secondary market) is sub-categorized into the First, Second, Third, and Fourth markets. This is the order of the development of these markets in the United States. The Fourth Market is direct trading of securities between institutions on the INSTINET system. (see INSTINET; ECN; compare First, Second, Third markets)

FRB   abbreviation for the Federal Reserve Board.

Freddie Mac   the commonly used name for securities issued by the Federal Home Loan Mortgage Corporation - a privatized government agency whose common stock trades on the NYSE. (see Federal Home Loan Mortgage Corporation)

Free credit balance   uninvested cash held in a customer's account. Broker-dealers must give a notice to each customer quarterly of the amount of such free credit balance, along with a statement that such funds are not segregated by the broker-dealer, and that the funds are payable to the customer on demand. (compare Credit balance)

Free riding   a prohibited practice where a customer buys securities and then does not pay on settlement, thus taking the brokerage firm for a "free ride."

Front running   a prohibited practice whereby an employee of a brokerage firm, prior to executing a large customer order, places the same order for his or her personal account - thus "front running" the customer.

Frozen account   a cash or margin account in which a customer has failed to meet a Regulation T margin call by "S + 2" (3 business day regular way settlement + 2 grace days = 5 business days after of the trade date). Such accounts are "frozen" for 90 days, requiring the customer to pay in advance for purchases; or deliver securities in advance of sales; during this period.

Fully diluted EPS   a calculation of earnings per share that assumes that all outstanding securities that can be converted into common shares (convertibles, rights, warrants, and employee stock options) have been converted; thereby increasing the number of outstanding shares over which the company's earnings must be distributed. This reduces ("dilutes") reported earnings per share (see Earnings per share, Dilution)

Fully registered bond   a bond where both the principal amount and the interest payments are registered in the name of the owner. All bonds issued in the U.S. are now fully registered. (compare Registered to principal only bond, Bearer bond)

Functional allocation   in an oil and gas program, a sharing arrangement where the limited partners bear the immediately deductible intangible drilling costs; while the general partner bears the tangible costs that must be recovered over a number of years (compare Disproportionate sharing arrangement, Overriding royalty interest, Net profits interest)

Fundamental analysis evaluating a company's balance sheet, income statement, management, marketing strategies, and research and development as a means of predicting the future, long-term price movement of its stock. Such an analysis is based on the "fundamentals" of the company. (compare Technical analysis)

Funded debt an archaic term used to describe very long term corporate bond issues (typically with at least 5 years to maturity) that are a "long term funding." Please note that this term is sometimes mistakenly applied to long term municipal bond issues.

Futures contracts to buy or sell commodities at a pre-determined "future" date. Commodities and commodities (futures) options are not securities and are not regulated by the SEC; rather the CFTC - Commodities Futures Trading Commission - regulates the futures markets.

FVX option the "Five Year Interest Rate Index" option traded on the CBOE, the FVX is based on the yield for 5-year Treasury Notes. The strike price is expressed in terms of yield. As interest rates rise, FVX calls go "in the money;" as interest rates fall, FVX puts go "in the money. The multiplier on the contract is 100.

G

GAN the abbreviation for a Grant Anticipation Note, this is a short term municipal obligation backed by expected federal grant monies to be received in the future for mass-transit, energy conservation and pollution control programs.

GDP the abbreviation for Gross Domestic Product, GDP is the total market value of goods and services produced in the United States in a year, excluding the value of production by U.S. owned overseas operations. (compare GNP)

General obligation (GO) bond commonly referred to as a G.O. bond, a municipal debt security that is backed by the full faith, credit, and taxing power of the municipality. For bonds of cities and towns, the interest and principal on the bond is usually paid out of ad valorem (property) taxes. For G.O. bonds issued by states, income and sales taxes are usually used to pay the debt service on the bonds. Because these bonds are "carried on the backs of the taxpayers," they are a non-self supporting debt. (compare Revenue bond, Self supporting debt)

General partner (GP) in a direct participation program (DPP) or limited partnership, the individual (or individuals) who manages the venture and who has unlimited financial liability should the DPP fail. (compare Limited partner)

General Principal a FINRA/NASD designation for a person who has passed the Series #24 examination, this individual is qualified to supervise all activities at a FINRA/NASD member firm.

Giftable the action of giving a gift to someone else. All possessions are "giftable."

Ginnie Mae the commonly used name for securities issued by the Government National Mortgage Association (GNMA). GNMA is the only government agency that is a purchaser of mortgages from primary lenders that is still backed by the unconditional guarantee of the U.S. Government.

Series #7 Glossary 83

Ginnie Mae pass-through   a debt instrument guaranteed by the Government National Mortgage Association that represents part of a pool of VA (Veterans Administration) and FHA (Federal Housing Administration) mortgages. GNMA buys VA and FHA mortgages from primary lenders, pools them, and sells undivided interests in the pool in the form of $25,000 face amount GNMA pass-through certificates. The monthly mortgage payments are "passed-through" to the certificate holders and consist of both principal and interest, with the interest portion being fully taxable. Ginnie Maes are directly guaranteed by the U.S. Government, whereas all other agency securities are not. (see Government National Mortgage Association (GNMA)

Glass Steagall Act   a federal law enacted in 1933 that separated commercial banking from investment banking, and which generally prohibited investment banks from owning commercial banks or from making commercial loans. This Act was repealed in late 1999 - now commercial banks and investment banks are free to combine and compete in each other's businesses.

Global fund   a mutual fund or closed-end fund that invests in the negotiable securities of corporations located in the U.S. and abroad.

GNP   abbreviation for Gross National Product, which is the sum of all goods and services produced by the U.S. economy in a year. GNP not only includes U.S. based production, but also includes the value of production by U.S. owned overseas operations. (compare GDP)

Good delivery   industry terminology for a dealer to dealer delivery of securities where the securities are in the proper form and amount; with all required documentation and signatures in good order

Good faith check   specified in the Official Notice of Sale for a new municipal bond issue, the amount of the cashier's or certified check which each underwriter must submit with its bid to the municipality. The checks belonging to the unsuccessful bidders are returned on the day the winning underwriter (lowest interest rate bid) is announced. The municipality keeps the check of the winning underwriter. When the bonds are printed with the winning interest rates and delivered, the balance due for the total amount of the issue is paid to the issuer by the underwriter.

Good til canceled   a time notation that can be placed on orders that are "away from the market" meaning that the order should remain open until it is either executed or expires. So-called "GTC" orders are subject to periodic renewal, so that old "stale" orders are not forgotten by a customer and then executed later in the market. (compare Day order)

Government National Mortgage Association   an agency of the U.S. government that buys Veterans Administration (VA) and Federal Housing Administration (FHA) insured mortgages from primary lenders, thereby providing them with more money to make loans. GNMA then places the mortgages that it has purchased into pools and issues certificates representing an undivided participation in each pool of mortgages. The monthly mortgage payments made into the pool are "passed-through" to the certificate holders, hence the name "mortgage backed pass through certificate." Monthly payments from Ginnie Maes consist of both interest and principal, the interest portion of which is fully taxable. GNMA is the only agency that is guaranteed by the U.S. Government; the other agencies (all have "Federal" in their name) are not directly government guaranteed.

Green shoe clause   a provision in the underwriting agreement between a corporate issuer and the underwriter that permits the underwriter to request up to 15% additional shares over the original size of an issue in response to strong investor demand for the new issue. It is named after the first company to use such a clause, the Green Shoe Company.

Gross domestic product abbreviated GDP, this is the total market value of goods and services produced in the United States in a year, excluding the value of production by U.S. owned overseas operations. (compare GNP)

Gross national product   abbreviated GNP, the sum of the value of all goods and services produced by the economy in a year, including the value of production by overseas subsidiaries of U.S. companies. (compare GDP)

Gross revenue pledge   a covenant found in a revenue bond contract and Trust Indenture under which revenues from a municipal revenue bond are promised to be allocated in the following sequence: 1) debt service; 2) operation and maintenance; 3) debt service reserve and; 4) operation and maintenance reserve account. It is called a "gross" revenue pledge because interest and scheduled principal repayment on the bonds are paid first, before all other expenses associated with the issue. Another name for this type of bond is a "gross lien revenue bond" - because the bondholders have claim to the gross revenues of the issuer, before any other payments are made. (see Flow of funds; compare Net revenue pledge)

Group net order   in the underwriting of a competitively bid new issue municipal bond, an order that is placed for the benefit of the syndicate account (group account). Also known as syndicate group orders, these are filled after pre-sale orders. (see Pre-Sale order, Priority provisions)

Growth fund   a management company (one of the 3 types of investment companies defined under the Investment Company Act of 1940) that buys common stocks (and equivalent securities such as convertibles) that have above average growth potential with the principal objective of achieving capital gains.

Growth investing   the selection of equity investments based solely on earnings or stock price growth over time, ignoring technical or fundamental factors. (compare Value investing)

Growth stock   stocks of new, expanding companies whose market values are expected to appreciate rapidly. A company whose common stock is described as a growth stock is usually characterized by a low dividend payout ratio and high retained earnings ratio. Such companies retain most of the earnings to fund future growth - the marketplace does not demand much of a dividend payout from such companies, because the value of the stock is appreciating.

GTC a time notation that can be placed on orders that are "away from the market" meaning "good-til-canceled." Subject to periodic renewal, the order remains in the market until it is executed or expires. (see Good til canceled, Open order; compare Day order)

Guaranteed bond a bond whose interest and principal payments are guaranteed by an entity other than the issuer. Corporate bonds of a subsidiary are typically guaranteed by the parent company; municipal industrial revenue bonds are guaranteed by the corporate lessee of the facility. Guaranteed bonds take on the (usually superior) credit rating of the guarantor.

Guaranteed preferred stock a preferred stock whose dividend payments are guaranteed by an entity other than the issuer. Typically, preferred stock issued by a subsidiary company will be guaranteed by the corporate parent; and takes on the usually superior credit rating of the corporate parent.

Guardian account a fiduciary account in which the court appoints a legal guardian to protect and manage the assets of a minor (such as a child that has been orphaned) or an incompetent adult. (see Fiduciary; compare Custodian account)

_H_

Head and shoulders top or bottom formation 1) a head and shoulders top formation is a stock price charting that depicts the stock's price moving upwards to a peak, and then trending downwards from that peak. Thus, this is an "uptrend" that is "reversing out;" 2) a head and shoulders bottom formation is a stock price charting that depicts the stock's price moving downwards to a trough, and then trending upwards from that bottom point. Thus, this is a "downtrend" that is "reversing out."

Hedge establishing a securities position that mitigates or decreases the market risk associated with a securities position that an investor already owns. For example, a long stock position can be hedged with the purchase of a put option (which allows the contract holder to "put" or sell the stock at a fixed price, even if the market declines). Do not confuse a "hedge" with a guarantee. Hedges to not guarantee against loss.

Hedge fund an unregistered investment company only open to accredited investors that employs aggressive strategies such as naked option selling and short sales to achieve higher returns (in return for the investor assuming higher risk).

Hedge fund of funds a registered investment company that makes investments in underlying hedge funds. (see Hedge fund)

Help Wanted Advertising Index a leading economic indicator published by the Conference Board that surveys the level of help wanted advertising in newspapers across the country - a high level indicates future employment gains and hence, greater economic output.

High yield bond also known as a "junk" bond, an issue that is below investment grade (that is, rated BB or lower) that pays a high rate of interest to compensate for the added credit risk.

Holder the term for the buyer of an option contract, also synonymous with being "long" the option contract. (compare Writer)

Holder of record   the person whose name appears as the owner of the security on the company's books as of the record date - thus, this person is entitled to receive any distributions made by the company. (see Record date)

Horizontal merger   a merger of 2 companies in the same businesses. For example, the merger of 2 automobile manufacturers is a horizontal merger. (compare Vertical merger)

Horizontal spread   an option spread position, where simultaneously the same type of option is bought and sold with the same strike price; and different expirations. When the positions are "stacked" one above the other, there is a no difference in the strike prices, but the expirations are different - on a time line, one expiration is longer than the other, hence the name horizontal spread. These are also called "calendar" spreads. (compare: Vertical spread, Diagonal spread)

Hot issue   a newly issued stock that immediately begins trading in the secondary market at a price higher than its initial offering price. Such an issue is "hot" in the market. (compare Sticky issue)

HR-10 plan   also called a Keogh plan, a retirement plan for self-employed individuals, based upon their self-employed income. Contributions to a Keogh are fully deductible from the employer's gross income. Employer contributions are limited to 50% of pre-deduction income annually, capped at a maximum of $46,000 (in 2008, increased from $40,000 in 2003) annual contribution. (see Defined Contribution Plan; compare Individual Retirement Account)

Hump shaped yield curve   an unusual yield curve shape that looks like a "hump shape," also called a bell shaped yield curve. In such a yield curve, yields for medium term maturities are higher than yields for both short term and longer term issues. This indicates a demand-supply imbalance in the medium term issues (their yields are higher than longer term issues due to lack or demand for; or an oversupply of; the medium term issues). (see Yield curve; compare Ascending yield curve; Inverted yield curve)

Hybrid market   the NYSE's newest trading system which gives customers the choice of filling their orders either through the SuperDOT system, that allows for price improvement by the Specialist but results in slower executions; or by using the Direct + system, which allows for pure electronic executions that are extremely fast, but which do not offer the possibility of price improvement.

Hypothecation   a customer's pledging of securities to a broker-dealer as collateral for a margin loan. (see Debit balance, Rehypothecation)

Hypothecation agreement   another term for a margin agreement, when a customer wishes to open a margin account, the customer must "hypothecate," that is , pledge, all of the securities in the account to the broker-dealer as collateral for the margin loan. This is accomplished by having the customer sign a hypothecation agreement, also called the margin agreement (and sometimes called the customer's agreement).

I

Immediate or cancel   abbreviated IOC on an order ticket, a notation on a contingency order instructing the floor broker to attempt to execute the entire order at one price in one try; however, if the broker can execute only part of this order, he must do so and then cancel the remainder of the order. The customer will accept the partial execution. (compare Fill or kill)

In the money   in option trading, a phrase that describes an option that has intrinsic value. Specifically, an option is "in-the-money" when the relationship between the market price of the underlying security and the strike price of the option is such that exercising would yield a profit to the holder (buyer), disregarding any premiums paid. A call is "in the money" when the market price of the underlying stock is greater than the call's strike price. A put is "in the money" when the market price of the underlying stock is lower than the put's strike price. (compare At the money, Out the money)

In-whole call   under the terms of the call covenant found in the bond contract, the issuer has the option of calling all of an outstanding issue at one time at predetermined dates and prices. The issuer will call in the bonds if interest rates have fallen sufficiently for the issuer to refinance at lower current rates and save on future interest payments. (compare Catastrophe call, Sinking fund call)

Income bond   a debt security that pays interest only if the company earns the interest or to the extent that the company earns the interest. Thus, the corporation must earn "income" in order for the payment to be made. This type of bond is usually issued by a corporation trying to reorganize its capitalization in order to avoid bankruptcy. With the bondholders' approval, the corporation would exchange its regular bonds for income (adjustment bonds). Income bonds trade flat (without accrued interest).

Income fund   a management company (one of the 3 types of investment companies defined under the Investment Company Act of 1940) with the investment objective of achieving high levels of income by purchasing bonds, preferred stocks and high dividend paying common stocks. To enhance returns, these funds also employ covered call writing and repurchase agreements.

Income oil and gas program   an oil and gas program that buys existing older wells, intending to "strip out" the remaining oil, with the oil revenue partly sheltered by the depletion deduction. Such programs employ "stripper" wells. (compare Exploratory oil and gas program, Developmental oil and gas program)

Income statement   a profit-and-loss statement showing all of the income and expenses of a business for a period of time. (compare Balance sheet)

Income stocks   equity securities (common and preferred stocks) that make regular and substantial dividend payments to shareholders, thus providing the investor with current cash. The securities may, or may not, have high long-term capital appreciation potential.

Income strategies   in options trading, any strategy in which the investor receives more options premium than he or she pays.

Indenture   a shortened wording for Trust Indenture, a series of covenants or protective promises made by the issuer of a debt security to the purchasers of a debt security. Typical covenants require the issuer to make semi-annual interest payments to the bondholder and to file annual reports with the SEC (for corporate bonds). To insure that the issuer complies with all of the terms of the covenants, an independent trustee is appointed by the issuer to protect the interest of the bondholders. The trustee is usually a commercial bank, that gives a report of its findings to the bondholders annually.

Index   a composite measure of the movement of the overall market or of a particular industry. Typically, an index consists of a large number of stocks and is usually weighted by other factors, such as capitalization, price, number of shares outstanding, etc. Among the most widely quoted indexes are the Dow Jones Industrial Average, which consists of 30 NYSE listed companies; and the Standard and Poor's 500 index, which consists of 500 stocks, composed principally of NYSE listed companies.

Index fund   a mutual fund that invests in a group of securities chosen to match the composition and weighting of a particular stock market index, such as the Standard and Poor's 500 Index, the New York Stock Exchange Composite Index, or the Value Line Index. Such funds track the performance of the index.

Index option   an option whose value is based on the movement of a stock index such as the Major Market Index, Standard and Poor's 100 Index, Standard and Poor's 500 index or the Dow Jones Industrial Average. Unlike a stock option, which can be exercised to acquire a fixed number of the underlying shares, exercise of an index option settles only in cash. (see Call option, Put option)

Indication of interest   during the 20-day "cooling off" period for a new non-exempt securities issue that is in registration under the Securities Act of 1933, orders to buy the issue cannot be solicited; however, underwriters are permitted to accept non-binding indications of interest from customers to get an idea of investor interest in the securities. see Cooling off period)

Individual retirement account (IRA)   a personal retirement plan that allows individuals with earned income to deposit up to $5,000 for the year 2008. Individuals age 50 or older can contribute an extra $1,000, for a total $6,000 contribution. Contributions are deductible in full for individuals who are not covered under another qualified retirement plan. If the individual is covered by another qualified retirement plan, the deductibility of the contribution varies with the individual's income. The earnings in the account accrue on a tax-deferred basis. (compare Education IRA, Roth IRA)

Industrial development bond (IDB)   a municipal revenue bond whose interest and principal payments are made from the proceeds of lease payments received from the corporation leasing the facility that is built with the proceeds of the bond issue. Under current tax law, this bond may be subject to the Alternative Minimum Tax (AMT) or regular tax. This type of bond can also be called an Industrial Revenue Bond.

Industrial revenue bond (IRB)   a municipal revenue bond whose interest and principal payments are made from the proceeds of lease payments received from the corporation leasing the facility that is built with the proceeds of the bond issue. Under current tax law, this bond may be subject to the Alternative Minimum Tax (AMT) or regular tax. This type of bond can also be called an Industrial Development Bond.

Inefficient market   a securities market that is characterized by low trading volumes and high transaction costs for effecting trades. This is the typical market for very thinly traded securities like direct participation programs and certain municipal bond issues. (compare Efficient market)

Inflation   a rise in the prices of goods and services that results when consumer demand increases relative to the supply of goods or services available. In short, there is too much money chasing too few goods; hence, prices rise. Inflation is most likely to occur when the economy is in a period of rapid expansion. (compare Deflation)

Initial margin requirement   set by the Federal Reserve Board under Regulation T, the percentage of a stock's market price that must be deposited when initially buying or selling short stock on margin. Currently the Regulation T margin requirement is 50% for both long and short stock positions. (see Regulation T; compare Minimum maintenance margin)

Initial public offering (IPO)   the first time that a company issues or sells its stock to the public. Such offerings must comply with the provisions of the Securities Act of 1933, unless an exemption is available. (compare Secondary offering)

Inside market the best market in a security, this is the highest current bid (highest price at which a dealer will buy) and lowest current ask (lowest current price at which a dealer will sell. (see Best market)

Insider defined under the Securities and Exchange Act of 1934, legally an officer, director, or 10% shareholder of a company. The definition has been extended by various court cases using Rule 10-b-5 (the "catch-all fraud rule") to include any person with material non-public information that may affect the market price of the security. Insiders are prohibited from trading based on this material non-public information, or from giving this information to another person if it results in a trade in that security, among other insider rules.

INSTINET acronym for Institutional Network, the electronic trading system that permits direct trades between institutions. It is also known as the fourth market. (see Fourth market; ECN)

Insurance covenant a promise made by a bond issuer in a bond contract to insure the facility built with the proceeds of the issue against loss. If the facility is destroyed, or damaged, then the insurance will pay for the repair or replacement of the facility so that it can continue to generate revenue to pay the debt service on the bonds.

Intangible asset also called intangibles on a balance sheet, the value of non-physical assets such as trademarks, copyrights, patents, goodwill, licenses, and franchises owned by the company. (compare Tangible asset)

Intangible drilling costs (IDC) in an oil and gas limited partnership, these are the costs of drilling for oil, including labor, fuel, and rental of drilling equipment that have no salvage value. Under current tax law, intangible drilling costs are 100% deductible as drilling occurs. (compare Tangible costs)

Interbank market the unregulated global market in which large foreign currency transactions occur between foreign and domestic banks. Trading in the interbank market determines the relative value of these currencies.

95

Interest rate   expressed as a percentage of the principal, the annual rate that is paid over the time that money is borrowed.

Interest rate option   options contracts traded on the CBOE, based on the yield of underlying U.S. Government securities. The strike price is expressed in terms of the interest rate. As interest rates rise, interest rate calls go "in the money;" as interest rates fall, interest rate puts go "in the money." The multiplier on the contracts is 100.

Interest rate risk   the risk that an increase in interest rates will result in lower bond prices. Interest rate risk for bonds is the same as market risk. (see Market risk)

Interested person   as defined under the Investment Company Act of 1940, a management company's Board of Directors cannot have more than 25% of its seats filled by "interested persons." These are individuals affiliated with the sponsor, custodian, transfer agent, or firms in the investment company's selling group.

Intermediation   the flow of funds into financial intermediaries (such as banks and savings and loans) by investors who are liquidating direct investments in securities. Intermediation occurs when the interest rate offered by banks to depositors is substantially higher than the interest rates available in the market for very safe investments, such as Treasury Bills. (compare Disintermediation)

Internal rate of return   in a direct participation program (DPP) offering, the computation of the real investment yield considering the time value of money; calculated by finding the implicit interest rate that discounts that program's projected annual cash flows to a present value of "0."

International fund   a mutual fund or closed-end fund that only invests in the negotiable securities of companies located outside the United States.

International Money Market the "IMM" is part of the Chicago Mercantile Exchange - a futures market that trades foreign currency futures and options on these futures. This market is regulated by the Commodities Futures Trading Commission (CFTC); not the Securities and Exchange Commission. Futures are not securities; nor are options on futures securities; hence they are not on the securities examinations.

Interpositioning a prohibited practice in which a broker-dealer uses a "middleman" firm in between itself and the contra-broker-dealer in a securities transaction. Using the middleman firm would add an extra commission or mark-up to the transaction. Doing so is prohibited under FINRA rules, unless it can be demonstrated that the use of the middleman firm results in a better price for the customer.

Intrastate offer an offer of securities that is made only in one state (as opposed to an interstate offer made in more than 1 state) that is an exempt transaction under the Securities Act of 1933, since the Federal government does not have jurisdiction unless the transaction crosses state lines. However, the offering must still be registered in that state, under the state "Blue Sky" laws.

Intrinsic value that portion of an option's premium reflecting the profit that exists to the contract holder from the difference between the market price of the underlying security and the strike price of an option, ignoring any premium paid by the holder. Call options, (and warrants) go "in the money" when the market price exceeds the exercise price. Put options go "in the money" when the market price is lower than the exercise price. Options that are "in the money" have intrinsic value. Options that are "at the money" or "out of the money" have no intrinsic value. (see In the money; compare At the money, Out the money)

Inventory turnover ratio the ratio of annual cost of goods sold to year-end inventory for a company. This ratio measures how quickly the company's inventory is being sold and replaced. The higher the ratio, the more efficient the company is at managing its inventory levels.

Inverted yield curve   a graph of the yields of fixed income securities of the same type (e.g., U.S. Governments or Corporates or Municipals) by maturity. As the maturity lengthens, the yield decreases, so the curve "descends." This is an unusual yield curve shape, that occurs when the Federal Reserve Board has tightened credit to slow down the economy. The Fed exerts its influence over short term rates, so its actions to tighten credit have increased short term rates above long term rates. (see Yield curve; compare Ascending curve, Normal yield curve)

Investment adviser   often called a portfolio manager, the financial professional who manages investment portfolios for investment companies, and for individual investors, charging a management fee for the services rendered. "IAs" must be registered with the Securities and Exchange Commission under the Investment Advisers Act of 1940; and must be registered in each state in which they operate under the state "Blue Sky laws.

Investment Advisers Act of 1940   the federal law, administered by the SEC, that requires investment advisers to mutual funds and advisers who manage $25,000,000 or more of assets to register with the SEC and file reports with the SEC. The other smaller advisers are only required to register with the State, not with the SEC.

Investment advisory services   SEC-registered companies or individuals who, for a fee, provide investment advice or money management, usually in specific types of investments.

Investment banker   also called an underwriter, a securities firm that assists issuers such as corporations or governments in raising capital by issuing securities.

Investment company   generic name for one of the companies formed under the Investment Company Act of 1940, whose primary business is investing and reinvesting in securities. These companies include mutual funds, closed-end funds, variable annuities, unit trusts, etc.

Investment Company Act of 1940   federal regulation administered by the SEC that defines the structure for investment companies (face amount certificate company; unit investment trust; or management company) and which sets the regulations under which the companies must operate.

Investment grade bond   any bond rated in the top 4 grades (AAA, AA, A and BBB) by Standard and Poor's, or rated Aaa to Baa Moody's. These ratings indicate bonds of the highest quality and lowest risk of default. (compare Junk bond)

IOC   abbreviation of immediate or cancel, a notation placed on an order to indicate that the customer wants the order executed at one price and at one time, but will accept the partial execution of the order. (compare AON, FOK)

IPO   abbreviation for Initial Public Offering, the first time that a company issues or sells its stock to the public. Such offerings must comply with the provisions of the Securities Act of 1933, unless an exemption is available. (compare Secondary offering)

IRA   a personal retirement plan that allows individuals with earned income to deposit up to $5,000 for the year 2008. Individuals age 50 or older can contribute an extra $1,000, for a total $6,000 contribution. Contributions are deductible in full for individuals who are not covered under another qualified retirement plan. If the individual is covered by another qualified retirement plan, the deductibility of the contribution varies with the individual's income. The earnings in the account accrue on a tax-deferred basis. (compare Education IRA, Roth IRA)

IRA rollover   a provision in the rules of Individual Retirement Accounts that allows an individual to "roll over" a distribution from any tax-qualified pension plan into an IRA within 60 days in order to avoid taxation. While a distribution can only be rolled over into an IRA once a year, there is no limit on the dollar amount that can be rolled over. Another type of rollover is permitted if a husband or wife inherits an IRA upon their spouse's death. This also avoids taxation until the beneficiary takes distributions from the account. (see Individual retirement account)

IRX option   the "Interest Rate Index" option traded on the CBOE, the IRX is based on the yield for 13-week Treasury Bills. The strike price is expressed in terms of yield. As interest rates rise, IRX calls go "in the money;" as interest rates fall, IRX puts go "in the money. The multiplier on the contract is 100.

Issued and outstanding   the portion of a company's authorized shares that have been distributed to investors, reduced by any repurchases of shares for the company's Treasury. These are the shares which are "outstanding" in the hands of the public and which trade in the market.

Issued stock   the number of shares out of the total authorized in the corporate charter that have actually been issued, i.e., sold to the public.

Issuer   a corporation, trust, partnership, or governmental unit or other legal entity that will issue securities

J

Joint account   an account owned by more than one individual, where all parties to the account sign a joint account agreement. Such accounts can be opened as Joint Tenants With Rights Of Survivorship (each party 100% owns the account); or Tenancy In Common (each party has a specified percentage ownership of the account). (see Joint account with rights of survivorship, Joint account with tenancy in common)

Joint account with tenants in common   an account in which each individual owns a divided interest. When one party dies, his or her specified interest or percentage of the account becomes part of the person's estate and can be willed to anyone. (compare Joint account with rights of survivorship)

Joint account with right of survivorship   a joint account in which each individual owns an undivided interest. Each person is, technically speaking, a 100% owner. When one party dies, the account is the sole property of the survivor(s); the deceased's interest in the account bypasses that person's estate. (compare Joint account with tenants in common)

Joint and last survivor annuity   an annuity option typically chosen by a husband and wife, where the annuity payment continues through the lives of both spouses. (compare Life annuity, Life with period certain annuity, Unit refund annuity)

Jumbo CD   a certificate of deposit having a denomination of $100,000 or more, this is a negotiable money market instrument that, unlike all other money market instruments which are original issue discount obligations, trades at par plus accrued interest. Also, unlike other money market instruments, these can have maturities greater than one year, can be callable, and the interest rate can be "resettable."

Junior lien bond   a secured corporate bond that is backed by a second mortgage on real property. These bonds have second claim (a "junior lien") to the collateral backing the bonds; the First mortgage (a "senior lien") bonds issued by the corporation have a prior claim. Mortgage bonds are typically issued by utilities. (compare Senior lien bond)

Junior security   a security whose claims on the assets and income of a company are lower than that of other securities. For example, common stock is junior to preferred stock in the liquidation of a company. (compare Senior security)

Junk bond   a low-quality, long-term bond rated BB (by Standard and Poor's) or Ba (by Moody's) or lower. These bonds are below investment grade and are considered to be speculative. Therefore, their yields are higher than investment grade debt. (compare Investment grade bond)

K

K-1   the tax reporting form sent annually by the general partner(s) to each limited partner that details the limited partner's share of income and loss from the venture for the tax year.

Keogh plan   also called an HR-10, a retirement plan for self-employed individuals, based upon their self-employed income. Contributions to a Keogh are fully deductible from the employer's gross income. Employer contributions are limited to 50% of pre-deduction income annually, capped at a maximum of $46,000 in 2008 (increased for inflation from the previous $40,000 limit in 2003). (see Defined Contribution Plan; compare Individual Retirement Account)

Keynesian theory   an economic theory postulated by John Maynard Keynes that the level of economic growth is determined by the level of fiscal stimulus provided by the government. (compare Monetarist theory, Supply-side theory)

Kiddie tax   a nickname for taxes imposed on custodian accounts, where the income under the tax code is taxed at the child's bracket. However, if the parent is the custodian; the child is age 18 or under; and the account has substantial income; then the income is taxed at the parent's (usually higher) bracket instead of the child's (usually lower) tax bracket.

L

L the broadest measure of the money supply, "L" includes money in all forms.

Laddering the selection of bonds into a portfolio with the maturities arranged to meet anticipated cash needs in the future - thus, the portfolio's maturities are "laddered." (compare Structuring)

Lagging economic indicator an economic measure that shows where the economy was in the business cycle during the past 12 months. Lagging indicators include reported corporate profits, the ratio of consumer credit to income levels, and employment duration. (compare Leading economic indicator, Coincident economic indicator)

LBO the acronym for Leveraged Buy Out, this is the purchase of all of the outstanding shares of a publicly traded company, with the monies used to purchase the shares coming from a bank loan; or the sale of long term bonds (hence the term Leveraged Buy Out). Once the company has been bought out, new management will reduce costs; and sell assets; to generate funds to pay down the debt incurred in the LBO.

Lead underwriter also called the managing or head underwriter, the investment banking firm that has the business relationship with the issuer of the securities. The lead underwriter forms the syndicate, drafts the syndicate agreement, acts on the syndicate's behalf, allocates the securities to each syndicate member and charges a management fee for its services. (see Agreement among underwriters)

Leading economic indicator one of the 10 economic measures that predict the future of the business cycle. Among the 10 are building permits, initial unemployment claims, stock prices, durable goods orders, and money supply levels. (compare Coincident economic indicator, Lagging economic indicator)

LEAP   acronym for Long-term Equity AnticiPation option, an exchange-traded, American-style stock option with a maximum 30 month life; or index option (most of which are European-style) with a maximum 36 month life; that enables the investor to take advantage of longer term trends than that permitted by the much shorter lived regular stock or index options. (see American-style option; compare European-style option)

Lease rental bond   a municipal revenue bond whose proceeds are used to build a facility which is leased to public and/or private users. The lease payments are used to pay the debt service (interest and principal) on the bond.

Legal list securities   a state-approved list of securities that can be purchased by commercial banks, savings and loans, pension plans, and for fiduciary accounts. This list typically consists of conservative, high-grade bonds and preferred stocks.

Legal opinion   the written opinion of the municipal bond attorney attesting to the fact that a municipal bond issue is valid, legal under the terms of the municipality's charter and that the interest on the bond is federally tax-exempt. An unqualified legal opinion means that the bond counsel has found no potential problems with the issue. A qualified legal opinion means that contingencies exist that could affect the bond's legal or tax status. (see Bond counsel)

Legislative risk   the risk that new laws, especially tax laws, will result in the decline in the value of a security. This is a particularly important risk consideration for tax advantaged investments such as municipal bonds and direct participation programs.

Letter of intent   1) in an underwriting, an agreement between an investment banker and the issuer of the security which details the basic terms of the underwriting - e.g., type of security, size of issue, estimated public offering price, compensation to the underwriter; 2) for mutual funds, an agreement that permits a mutual fund purchaser, who is approaching a breakpoint, to take advantage of a reduced sales charge by agreeing to pay for additional securities at a later date. A letter of intent for a mutual fund purchase must be completed within 13 months of the date of the letter; and can be backdated for up to 90 days. (see Breakpoint)

Letter security   an unregistered stock or bond that is sold privately by the issuer, typically under a Regulation D private placement exemption. The purchaser must sign a letter stating that the purchase is being made for investment only and that he or she does not intend to resell the security in the public markets (since these securities have not been registered with the SEC). (see Regulation D)

Level debt service   a serial bond structure, similar to a mortgage repayment schedule, that provides for equal annual payments to be made by the issuer to repay a debt; with part of the payment being interest, and part being a principal repayment. In the earlier years, more of the level payment consists of interest; in the later years, more of the level payment consists of principal repayment.

Leverage   1) the purchase (or sale) of a large amount of a security using a large percentage of borrowed money - e.g., buying stock on margin; 2) the portion of a company's long term capital that was raised from selling debt (as opposed to selling stock in the company).

Leveraged buy out (LBO)   the purchase of all of the outstanding shares of a publicly traded company, with the monies used to purchase the shares coming from a bank loan; or the sale of long term bonds (hence the term Leveraged Buy Out). Once the company has been bought out, new management will reduce costs; and sell assets; to generate funds to pay down the debt incurred in the LBO.

Liability   on a balance sheet, a claim on a company's assets which must be paid at some future date. (see Current liability, Long-term liability)

LIBOR   the abbreviation for "London Interbank Offered Rate," LIBOR is the interest rate charged on overnight loans of Eurodollars (basically the European equivalent of "Fed Funds" - short term loans of reserves from bank to bank).

Life annuity   an annuity option where payments are made to the annuitant for his or her entire life; when that person dies, payments stop. (compare Life annuity with period certain, Joint and last survivor annuity, Unit refund annuity)

Life annuity with period certain   an annuity option where payments are made to the annuitant for life; however after the annuity begins, if the person dies before a fixed amount of time has passed (usually, 10 years - so there is a 10 year "period certain"), the annuity will continue to make payments to a designated beneficiary through that fixed period. (compare Life annuity, Joint and last survivor annuity, Unit refund annuity)

Life cycle fund   a mutual fund that automatically rebalances as the customer ages, shifting asset allocations to less risky asset classes as the customer gets older.

LIFO   acronym for Last In, First Out, an accounting practice whereby; 1) the most recently acquired inventory is the first to be sold; 2) for tax accounting, the last transaction to occur results in the first tax event when the securities giving rise to the transaction are sold or payments are taken that result from that transaction. (compare FIFO)

Like kind exchange   an IRS rule that allows the sale of an asset, and the subsequent purchase of a "substantially similar" asset, without having a "tax event" - that is there is no capital gain or loss computation required for tax purposes.

Limit order   an order to buy a security (buy limit) at a specified price or lower, or to sell a security (sell limit) at a specified price or higher. A buy limit order is placed below the current market price of the security, and is executed if the market falls to, or through, that price. A sell limit order is placed above the current market price of the security, and is executed if the market rises to, or through, that price. (compare Stop order)

Limited partner (LP)   in a direct participation program (DPP) or limited partnership, the individuals who provide the capital for the venture and who have no say in the day-to-day management of the partnership. They are the passive investors. Their liability is limited to their cash contribution as well as any recourse loans. (see Recourse loan; compare General Partner)

Limited partnerships   more commonly known as a direct participation program ("DPP") or tax shelter, this is a partnership that permits the gains and losses of the business to flow through from the program to the investors (known as limited partners) untaxed. The partners include the items of income and loss on their individual tax returns, and hence directly participate in the results of the enterprise. (see Direct participation programs, Tax shelters)

Limited tax bond   a general obligation municipal bond on which a limit is placed on the issuer's ability to increase taxes in order to pay off the bond. This is a very rare (if not non-existent, type of G.O. bond issue). (see General Obligation bond; compare Unlimited tax bond)

Liquidity risk   the risk that effecting a securities transaction will result in larger than normal transaction costs. Liquidity risk increases for securities that are thinly traded, meaning that they are difficult to trade. (compare Marketability risk)

Listed option   a call or put option that trades on a registered exchange. The options exchanges are the Chicago Board Options Exchange (CBOE); American Stock Exchange (AMEX); Philadelphia Stock Exchange (PHLX); Pacific Stock Exchange (PAC), now renamed the ARCA Exchange after its purchase by NYSE-owned Archipelago; and the International Securities Exchange (ISE).

Listed stock   a company whose stock meets the listing requirements of one of the exchanges and therefore trades on the "floor" of the exchange. Note that in the NASDAQ Stock Market there is no physical trading "floor" - just a computer trading network, however the term "listed" applies to companies listed on NASDAQ as well.

Load   the sales charge that an investor pays when buying a mutual fund share.

Load fund   a mutual fund that charges its purchasers a sales charge when they purchase or redeem shares of the fund. (compare No-load fund)

Loan consent agreement   usually signed when opening a margin account, the customer gives the broker-dealer the right to loan his or her securities to other customers for short sales. (see Margin agreement, Short sale)

Loan value   in a margin account, the portion of the market value of a security that can be lent to a customer. With a Regulation T margin requirement of 50% for stocks; these securities have a loan value of 50%. If Regulation T margin were 60% for stocks; these securities would have a loan value of 40%.

London interbank offered rate   abbreviated as "LIBOR," this is the interest rate charged on overnight loans of Eurodollars (basically the European equivalent of "Fed Funds" - short term loans of reserves from bank to bank).

Long   buying or owning a security.

Long bond   generally speaking, a bond with a maturity greater than ten years. Specifically relating to U.S. Government bonds, the "Long bond" is the 30-year maturity issue. Issuance of long bonds was discontinued by the Treasury in 2001, and resumed in February of 2006. (compare Medium term bond, Short bond)

Long call   an option contract to buy stock (or another underlying security) at a fixed price, good until a fixed expiration date, purchased by an investor. (compare Short call)

Long call spread   the purchase of a lower strike price call option; and the sale of a higher strike price call option; on the same underlying security. This is a bull market strategy. In a rising market, there is a profit on the long call (lower strike) that ultimately is limited by the higher strike short call. Spreads are gain limiting and loss limiting positions. (compare Short call spread)

Long margin account   a margin account in which a customer buys securities on margin. (compare Short margin account)

Long market value   the market value of securities that are bought in a margin account. The value of these securities is marked to market daily. (see Mark to market, Long margin account)

Long position   phrase denoting ownership of a security, that includes the right to transfer ownership and to participate in the rise and fall of its market value. (compare Short position)

Long put   an option contract that allows the holder to sell common stock (or another underlying instrument) at a fixed price, good until a fixed expiration date. (compare Short put)

Long put spread   the purchase of a higher strike price put option; and the sale of a lower strike price put option; on the same underlying security. This is a bear market strategy, also termed a Bear Put Spread. In a falling market, the long put with the higher strike goes "in the money" first for a profit. If the market keeps dropping, the lower strike price short put also goes "in the money," limiting potential gain to the difference in the strike prices (net of the premium paid). Spreads are gain limiting and loss limiting positions. (compare Short put spread)

Long sale   the sale of a security that is owned by a customer, where the customer will deliver that security to the broker on settlement date. The customer receives the proceeds from the long sale of the securities. (compare Short sale)

Long spread   an option spread in which the investor simultaneously buys the option with the higher premium and sells the same type of option with the lower premium. The net difference between the higher premium paid and the lower premium received is the debit. This type of spread is profitable if the difference between the premiums widens. If it is a vertical (price) debit spread, this position is profitable, as well, if both positions are exercised (see Spread, compare Short spread)

Long straddle   the purchase of a call and a put option on the same underlying security, with the same strike price and expiration. This option strategy is used when it is expected that the market will be volatile. (compare Short straddle)

Long term capital gain (loss)   a gain or loss upon disposition of an asset that has been held for over 1 year. Long term capital gains are taxed at lower tax rates than short term capital gains - assets held over 12 months are taxed at a maximum rate of 15%. (see Short term capital gain (loss))

Long term liability   more commonly called long-term debt on the balance sheet, any liability that is payable in more than one year. Typically this would be the principal amount on any long term outstanding debt. (compare Current liability)

M

M   following a number, this letter denotes 1,000 - e.g., $50M means $50,000 (M comes from the Latin numbering system, where M = 1,000).

M1   a measure of the money supply, this is cash in circulation and demand (checkable) deposits.

M2   a broader measure of the money supply than M1 (currency in circulation and checkable deposits), M2 equals M1 plus time deposits of less than $100,000.

M3   a broader measure of the money supply than M2 (currency in circulation and checkable deposits and time deposits of less than $100,000), M3 equals M2 plus time deposits of more than $100,000.

Maintenance call   a demand from a broker that an investor deposit enough cash or securities in a margin account to restore the account to the minimum maintenance margin. (see Minimum maintenance margin)

Maintenance covenant   a promise made by a municipal revenue bond issuer to maintain the facility built with the proceeds of the issue in good repair (so it can continue to generate revenues).

Maintenance margin   another term for minimum maintenance margin, set by the NYSE and the NASD (now merged into FINRA), the minimum equity that a customer must maintain in a margin account. Below this percent or amount the customer gets a maintenance call to restore the equity in the account to the minimum maintenance margin. Minimum maintenance margins are currently 25% for long stock positions and 30% for short stock positions (with some exceptions). (compare Initial margin requirement)

Major Market Index option   an index option that mimics the Dow Jones Industrial Average, it consists of 20 stocks in different industries, and is traded on the American Stock Exchange under the symbol XMI.

Managed offering   the underwriting of a limited partnership in which the issuer retains an underwriter to "manage" the sale of the issue to the public. The underwriter sells partnership units under a firm commitment and earns a spread. (see Firm commitment; compare Non-managed offering)

Management company   one of the three types of investment companies defined under the Investment Company Act of 1940. This investment company is organized as a corporation and employs an investment adviser to manage a portfolio of securities, against which it issues shares to the public. Depending on how it issues securities to the public, a management company is described as either an open-end management company (i.e., a mutual fund) or a closed-end management company (i.e., a publicly traded fund). (see Open end fund, Closed end fund)

Management fee   1) in an underwriting, the fee charged by the managing underwriter for acting on behalf of the syndicate. (see Managing Underwriter); 2) in investment companies, a percentage of a fund's total assets that the fund's portfolio manager or investment adviser charges annually for making investment decisions. This is typically the largest expense of operating a mutual fund.

Managing underwriter   also called the lead or head underwriter, the investment banking firm that has the business relationship with the issuer of the securities. The managing underwriter forms the syndicate, drafts the syndicate agreement, acts on the syndicate's behalf, allocates the securities to each syndicate member and charges a management fee for its services. (see Agreement among underwriters)

Mandatory call   a call provision in a bond contract that requires an issuer to call in the bonds, usually by putting extra money into the sinking fund each year, that will be used to retire some of the outstanding bonds by a "random pick" at preset dates. In lieu of calling in the bonds at these dates, the issue can retire bonds using the monies in the sinking fund to purchase them in the open market (if this is cheaper). (compare Optional call)

Margin account   an account defined under Regulation T in which a customer buys or sells short securities by depositing cash equal to part of the securities' market value. The Regulation T initial margin requirement for such positions is 50% for both long and short stock positions. Only "marginable securities," as defined under Regulation T, can be purchased or sold short in a margin account. (see Long margin account, Short margin account, Margin security)

Margin agreement   also called a hypothecation agreement, the document an investor must sign when opening a margin account. By signing it, the investor pledges the securities he or she purchases in the account as collateral for the margin loan. The agreement also details the terms of the margin loan, including the interest rate and how the loan balance will be computed. In addition to the margin agreement, it is customary for the customer in a margin account to sign a loan consent agreement. (see Loan consent agreement)

Margin call   a demand from a brokerage firm for an investor to deposit enough cash (or securities) in a margin account to meet either the Regulation T initial margin requirement, or to restore the account to minimum maintenance margin following an adverse price move. A call for initial margin is sometimes referred to as a Fed call. (see Initial margin requirement, Maintenance call)

Margin department   part of a brokerage firm's operations department or "back office" that is responsible for making sure that all accounts (cash accounts, as well as margin accounts) are maintained under margin and account regulations of the Federal Reserve Board (FRB), and the self-regulatory organizations such as the NYSE and NASD (now merged into FINRA). The margin department maintains all customer account records, generates account statements; computes an investor's equity in both cash and margin accounts daily; and sends out margin calls as appropriate.

Margin requirement   the percentage of the purchase price of a security that must be deposited to buy (or sell short) on credit. Regulation T of the Federal Reserve Board sets initial margins at 50% for both long and short stock positions.

Margin security   also called a marginable security, a stock or bond that can be bought or sold in a margin account. Among registered stocks these include all those listed on exchanges, all NASDAQ stocks, and any over-the-counter stock that appears on the Federal Reserve Board's OTC margin list.

Mark to market   industry phrase for the process by which a brokerage firm computes the value of the shares in an investor's account based on the daily closing price.

Mark-down   the amount or percentage that is subtracted from the bid price when a customer sells an OTC stock to a market maker in a principal transaction. There is no requirement to disclose the mark-down amount in principal transactions in non-NASDAQ securities. Under the FINRA/NASD 5% Policy, mark-downs (and mark-ups) must be fair and reasonable. (see Principal transaction; compare Commission)

Mark-up   the amount or percentage that is added to the inside ask price when a customer buys an OTC security from a FINRA/NASD member firm acting as a principal or market maker in the transaction. Except for NASDAQ stocks, the mark-up on an OTC principal transaction is not usually disclosed to the customer on a confirmation; rather it is included in a net price to the customer. (see Mark-down; compare Commission)

Market discount bond   a bond issued at par, that is trading for less than par in the market. Bonds trade at discounts to par either because market interest rates have risen after issuance; or the credit quality of the bond has deteriorated. (compare Market premium bond)

Market expectations theory   a theory explaining the shape of the yield curve that states that the shape of the curve shows interest rate movements that are expected in the future - e.g., an ascending curve shows that interest rates are expected to rise in the future; a descending curve shows that interest rates are expected to fall in the future. (see Yield curve)

Market index linked CD   a certificate of deposit whose return is based on the S&P 500 Index return rather than on money market interest rates.

Market maker   synonymous with an OTC dealer, a FINRA/NASD member firm that disseminates bid and ask prices at which it stands ready to buy stock into, and sell stock from, its inventory at its own risk in the over-the-counter market. On the stock exchanges, the Specialist performs the function of market maker, as well as handling the book of public orders. On the CBOE, the market maker maintains bid and ask prices in options contracts.

Market order   an order to buy or sell a security immediately at the best available market price. Market orders have first priority on an exchange floor. (compare Limit order; Stop order)

Market out clause   a provision in the Letter of Intent entered into between the underwriter and the issuer, that allows the underwriter to terminate the underwriting commitment if unforeseen, calamitous events occur, such as an act of war. (see Letter of Intent)

Market premium bond   a bond issued at par, that is trading for more than par in the market. Bonds trade at premiums to par either because market interest rates have fallen after issuance; or the credit quality of the bond has improved. (compare Market discount bond)

Market risk   1) for equity securities, the risk that the value of the stocks will drop due to a sell-off in the market; 2) for bonds, the risk that a rise in interest rates will cause the market prices of bonds to drop (see Interest rate risk); 3) in portfolio management, the risk inherent in a portfolio that cannot be diversified away. (see Systematic risk)

Market value   the price of a security determined by the forces of supply and demand in the market place.

Marketability risk   the risk that a securities position will be difficult to liquidate - e.g., it is not very marketable. Marketability risk is greatest for thinly traded securities like direct participation programs. Marketability risk is also rather high for municipal bonds. (compare Liquidity risk)

Marketable securities   securities for which there are active markets. These securities can be bought and sold easily, and have low marketability risk.

Married put   when a customer buys a put and buys the underlying stock at the same time. The result is a hedged stock position. For tax purposes, when a put is married to the stock, the stock's holding period counts normally. If the put were purchased on another day after the stock was purchased (if the stock had been held short term at that time), then the stock's holding period stops counting as of the date of the put purchase and reverts to "0." Thus, the stock's holding period stays short term, and such a strategy cannot be used to "stretch" a short term capital gain into a long term capital gain.

Master limited partnership   a limited partnership (tax shelter) investment that actually trades on an exchange or over-the-counter, just like a stock. These investments came out in the mid 1980s; and as of today, are pretty much defunct due to tax law changes.

Matched sale   another term for a Reverse repurchase agreement. (see Reverse repurchase agreement)

Maturity date   the date on which the borrower must to repay the principal on an outstanding debt security.

MBIA   abbreviation for Municipal Bond Insurance Association Corp., a company to which a municipality pays a fee to insure the timely payment of interest and principal on a bond issue. This "insurance" results in a better credit rating and lower interest cost for the issuer. (see AMBAC, FGIC, BIGI)

Medallion signature guarantee program   to transfer ownership of a stock certificate, the "assignment" (customer signature) must be guaranteed. The transfer agent will accept the guarantee of any "Medallion" member - these are mainly commercial banks and FINRA member firms.

Medium-term bond   generally speaking, a bond maturing in two to ten years. (compare Long bond, Short bond)

Member order   in the underwriting of a new issue municipal bond, an order from a syndicate member to buy the bonds for that member's own account or a related portfolio. Also called member takedown orders, these are the last orders to be filled under the priority provisions. (see Priority provisions; compare Pre-Sale order, Group order, Designated order)

Merger   the joining of two companies either under friendly or hostile terms. Investment bankers advise companies on the terms of such merger agreements. A horizontal merger is where 2 companies in the same business merge; a vertical merger is where 2 companies in different businesses merge.

MIG   acronym for Moody's Investment Grade, the designation used by Moody's Investor Service to rate short term municipal notes. The acronym is followed by a number that indicates the note's quality, with 1 indicating the highest quality (MIG 1), descending to MIG 2, MIG 3, and SG (Speculative Grade).

Mill rate   also called millage rate, the rate of ad valorem taxation in a municipality. One mill is equal to .001 or one-tenth of 1%. (see Ad valorem taxes)

Mineral rights cost   the price paid by a partnership for the right to extract minerals, such as oil and gas, from the ground.

Mini-maxi commitment   a type of best efforts underwriting commitment in which the investment banker makes an all or none commitment on a minimum amount of the new issue and a best efforts commitment to continue selling more of the issue until a maximum specified amount is sold. (see All-or-none commitment, Best efforts commitment)

Minimum maintenance margin   set by the NYSE and the NASD (now merged into FINRA), the minimum equity that a customer must maintain in a margin account. Below this percent or amount, the customer gets a maintenance call to restore the equity in the account to the minimum maintenance margin. Minimum maintenance margins are currently 25% for long stock positions and 30% for short stock positions (with some exceptions.) (compare Initial margin requirement)

MKT   abbreviation for an order to be filled "at the market price." Market orders have priority over all other orders.

MM   following a number, this letter denotes 1,000,000 - e.g., $50MM means $50,000,000. (compare M)

Monetarist theory   an economic theory postulated by Milton Friedman that the level of economic growth is determined by monetary policy, that is, the actions the Federal Reserve Board. (compare Keynesian theory, Supply-side theory)

Monetary environment   the level of interest rates in the economy and the expectation for future interest rate levels based on monetary and fiscal policy actions. (see Fiscal policy, Monetary policy)

Monetary policy   actions taken by the Federal Reserve Board (FRB) to loosen or tighten the money supply. These actions include engaging in open market operations, changing the discount rate, changing the reserve requirement, changing margin requirements, and moral suasion. (see Moral suasion; compare Fiscal policy)

Money market instrument   debt obligations that mature in less than one year, such as certificates of deposit, commercial paper, or banker's acceptances. These will turn into "money" within the year, hence the name. (compare Capital market instrument)

Money market mutual fund   an open-end management company that invests in short-term, low-risk money market instruments such as Treasury Bills and Commercial Paper. There is no sales charge to invest in a money market mutual fund - these are no-load funds.

Money market preferred   adjustable rate preferred whose dividend is adjusted to reflect short-term interest rates of money market instruments such as Treasury bills and commercial paper.

Money market securities   short-term, highly liquid debt securities such as U.S Government Treasury bills, corporate commercial paper, banker's acceptances, negotiable certificates of deposit, and Federal funds. Money market securities mature within 1 year; though the majority of issues have much shorter maturities than this.

Money multiplier   since a bank is only required to maintain a portion (typically 20%) of money deposited (the "Reserve Requirement"), 80% of that amount may be reloaned. When this 80% is deposited in another bank, again, the bank must maintain a portion (20%) and may reloan the balance. As money is loaned and deposited from bank to bank to bank, the original deposit amount "multiplies" to a much greater amount of credit. This ultimately results in the creation of a larger amount of credit, and is known as the "money multiplier." (see Reserve requirement)

Money purchase plan   a defined contribution retirement plan that specifies a fixed percentage of income or fixed dollar amount to be contributed into the plan annually.

Money supply   the amount of money that is available in the economy. In the simplest terms, it includes M1 (all money in circulation and in checkable accounts); M2 (M1 plus all money in savings accounts and time deposits of $100,000 or less) as well as money market mutual funds); M3 (M2 plus time deposits over $100,000); and L: M3 plus money market instruments and government savings bonds.

Moody's Investors Service   one of the independent companies that rate the risk of default and the quality of the cash flow or assets backing fixed income issues - bonds, preferred stocks, and commercial paper. The three ratings services include (from largest to smallest) Moody's Investors Service, Standard and Poor's, and Fitch's.

Moral obligation bond   a municipal bond whose terms state that if revenues or tax collections are insufficient to meet debt service requirements, then the state legislature has a moral obligation, but not a legal obligation, to apportion the funds to pay the debt service on the issue.

Moral suasion   "jawboning" actions by the Chairman of the Federal Reserve to induce member banks to either expand or contract their lending levels.

Mortality guarantee   a guarantee made by an insurance company to an annuity purchaser that the annuitant will receive the annuity payments throughout his or her entire life, no matter how long he or she lives. (compare Expense guarantee)

Mortgage bond   a secured corporate bond that is backed by specific real estate the company owns. The bondholder, in effect, has a lien on the company's real estate. The major issuers of mortgage bonds are public utilities. (see Open-end mortgage bond, Closed-end mortgage bond)

Mortgage REIT   a highly leveraged Real Estate Investment Trust that makes construction loans to builders and mortgage loans to buyers of real estate. Mortgage REITS also buy various CMO tranches for investment. The REIT profits from the difference between the lower interest rate at which it borrows money and the higher interest rate it earns on construction and mortgage loans and CMO investments. (compare Equity REIT)

Mortgage-backed securities (MBS)   securities that are backed by mortgages, typically issued by government agencies such as GNMA (Government National Mortgage Association); FNMA (Federal National Mortgage Association); and FHLMC (Federal Home Loan Mortgage Corporation). The securities are "pass-through" certificates that represent an undivided interest in a pool of mortgages assembled by the agency. Each month, the pro-rata portion of the monthly mortgage payment is "passed-through" to the certificate holder.

MSRB   abbreviation of the Municipal Securities Rulemaking Board which was established in 1975 as the primary rulemaking authority for the municipal market participants which include banks and broker-dealers.

Multiple   the number of times annual earnings at which a common stock is valued in the market.

Multiplier   a term used for index option contracts, where there is no physical underpinning of a fixed number of securities that must be bought or sold if the contract is exercised. Instead of the contract covering 100 shares, the contract is said to have a "multiplier" of 100.

Munibase   a municipal bond database published by J. J. Kenny and Co, it gives the relevant details of all outstanding municipal issues (e.g., issue date, maturities, coupon rates, etc.)

Municipal bond   a debt security issued by a municipality, state, political subdivision, authority, or territory of the United States.

Municipal note   a municipal security issued with a short term maturity (generally 90 days or less); though there are some municipal notes, such as CLNs - Construction Loan Notes - that have longer maturities. (see Bond anticipation note, Construction loan note, Revenue anticipation note, Tax anticipation note, Tax and revenue anticipation note)

Municipal Securities Principal   an MSRB license designation for an individual who has passed the Series #53 examination. This person can supervise all activities of a municipal securities firm.

Munifacts wire   owned by The Bond Buyer, a wire service that primarily disseminates market information about the price and allocation of new municipal bond offerings. Current events affecting the secondary market for municipal bonds are also distributed over Munifacts. (see Bond buyer)

Mutual fund   the commonly used name for an open-end management company that establishes a diversified portfolio of investments that is actively managed, and then continually issues new shares and redeems old shares representing ownership in the portfolio. (see Open-end fund)

N

Naked option   also termed an uncovered option, a short call or put option position that is unprotected against its maximum possible loss in the market. Thus, the writer of the contract (the seller of the option) is "exposed" to market risk, hence the term "naked option." The writer of a naked option must deposit margin in order to establish the position. (compare Covered option)

Narrow based index option   an index option contract based on a stock index that includes issuers in only one industry or country. (compare Broad based index option)

NASD   abbreviation for the National Association of Securities Dealers, the self-regulatory body of the over-the-counter market established in 1938 under the Maloney Act amendments to the Securities Exchange Act of 1934. In 1996, the NASD was split into 2 entities - the NASDAQ Stock Market; and NASD Regulation Inc. The NASDAQ Stock Market is the operator of the marketplace; while NASD Regulation is an independent enforcer of NASD rules. In mid-2007, NASD Regulation was merged with NYSE Regulation into a new single regulator - FINRA - Financial Industry Regulatory Authority.

NASDAQ   acronym for National Association of Securities Dealers Automated Quotation system, an inter-dealer computer system that provides brokers, traders, and market makers with current bid and asked quotes for OTC securities. This is now simply called the NASDAQ Stock Market. The NASDAQ system also allows for automated trade execution for these securities via SingleBook (which incorporates the predecessor SuperMontage and SuperSOES systems) for both NASDAQ Global Market issues and NASDAQ Capital Market issues).

NASDAQ Index   the broadest measure of over-the-counter trading, this weighted index includes all of the approximately 3,200 issues that trade on the NASDAQ system. (see NASDAQ)

NASDAQ Level I   the first level of the NASDAQ system, it displays the inside market for the security. This level is intended for use by registered representatives. (see Inside market; compare NASDAQ Level II, NASDAQ Level III)

NASDAQ Level II   intended for use by OTC trading desks, NASDAQ Level II displays the quotes of all market makers in NASDAQ issues, with the quote size. (compare NASDAQ Level I, NASDAQ Level III)

NASDAQ Level III   intended for use by market makers, this NASDAQ level displays the quotes from all dealers with the quote size; and allows dealers to change their own quote. (compare NASDAQ Level I, NASDAQ Level II)

NASDAQ Global Market issues   the NASDAQ Stock Market is divided into NASDAQ Global Market issues and NASDAQ Capital Market issues. The larger stocks (about 2800 out of 3200 NASDAQ stocks) are included in the Global Market - this is NASDAQ's competitor for a NYSE listing. The 400 or so smaller NASDAQ stocks are included in the Capital Market listing.

NASDAQ Stock Market   a negotiated trading market using a network of market makers located throughout the United States to trade mainly smaller and high technology issues (also known as the "over-the-counter" market)

Negotiable certificate of deposit   a certificate of deposit having a denomination of $100,000 or more, this is a negotiable money market instrument that, unlike all other money market instruments which are original issue discount obligations, trades at par plus accrued interest. Also, unlike other money market instruments, these can have maturities greater than one year, can be callable, and the interest rate can be "resettable."

Negotiable security   a security that can be bought or sold (traded), usually without restriction, and whose title can be easily transferred when it is traded. (compare Redeemable security)

Negotiated market a securities market where traders "negotiate" a price - this is the trading method for the OTC market. (compare Auction market)

Negotiated underwriting used for virtually all new issues of corporate securities and municipal revenue bonds, a type of underwriting in which the issuer and the underwriting negotiate all of the terms of the letter of intent and subsequent underwriting. (compare Competitive bid underwriting)

Net asset value (NAV) the value of each share of a management company which is computed by totaling the current market value of each security held in the fund portfolio and subtracting the fund's liabilities to find Total Net Assets. Total Net Assets is divided by the total number of outstanding shares. to get NAV per share. Management companies (both open-end and closed-end) compute NAV at the end of each trading day.

Net capital the minimum liquid net worth that must be maintained by a broker-dealer in order for the firm to operate. The SEC sets the minimum net capital requirements under the Net Capital Rule.

Net direct debt the direct debt of a municipality minus any self-supporting debt such as revenue bonds; and minus any payments that have been made into its sinking fund. This represents the "net" amount of debt directly issued by that municipality that is the responsibility of the taxpayers in that jurisdiction. (see Direct debt, Self-supporting debt)

Net interest cost in a competitive bid underwriting where the lowest interest rate bid wins, the computation of the weighted average interest cost to the issuer without considering the time value of money. (compare True interest cost)

Net overall debt for a municipality, the total of Net Direct debt plus Overlapping debt. Net overall debt is then compared to the population of the municipality to get a debt per capita figure in order to measure the municipality's creditworthiness. (see Net direct debt, Overlapping debt)

Net profits interest   in an oil and gas program. a sharing arrangement where the general partner gets a percentage of defined "net profits," which usually excludes any intangible drilling costs incurred. (compare Disproportionate sharing arrangement, Functional allocation, Overriding royalty interest)

Net revenue pledge   a covenant found in a revenue bond contract and Trust Indenture under which revenues from a municipal revenue bond are promised to be allocated in the following sequence: 1) operation and maintenance; 2) debt service; 3) debt service reserve and; 4) operation and maintenance reserve account. It is called a "net" revenue pledge because interest and scheduled principal repayments on the bonds are paid from the net revenues that remain after operation and maintenance expenses are paid. (see Flow of funds; compare Gross revenue pledge)

Net tangible assets   all assets of a company except for intangibles such as copyrights and patents, equals the tangible assets of a company. Netting out all liabilities of a company from this amount equals net tangible assets.

Net transaction   a transaction, such as the purchase of a new issue, in which the buyer is not charged a commission. The buyer is charged a "net" price inclusive of any spread to the underwriter.

Net working capital   the excess of current (liquid) assets over current liabilities.

Net worth   1) also called stockholder's equity, the excess of a company's total assets over and above its total liabilities on the balance sheet; 2) the difference between the total value of a person's assets and possessions - e.g., home, land, savings accounts, investments, etc. - and that person's total indebtedness - e.g., home mortgage, credit card debt, school loans, etc.

Network A   the part of the Consolidated Tape that reports trades of all NYSE-listed stocks, no matter where the trade occurred. The tape runs during regular NYSE trading hours - 9:30 AM-4:00 PM Eastern time; and the seller must report each trade to the tape within 90 seconds of execution. (see Consolidated tape)

Network B the part of the Consolidated Tape that reports trades of all American Stock Exchange listed stocks. The tape runs during regular AMEX trading hours - 9:30 AM-4:00 PM Eastern time; and the seller must report each trade to the tape within 90 seconds of execution. (see Consolidated tape)

Network C the part of the Consolidated Tape that reports trades of all NASDAQ listed stocks. The tape runs during regular NASDAQ trading hours - 9:30 AM - 4:00 PM Eastern Time; and the seller must report each trade to the tape within 90 seconds of execution.

New account form the document, completed by the registered representative, that details the name, address, social security number, occupation and employer, and citizenship of a new customer (among other items). On the form, a suitability determination for that customer is also documented.

New Housing Authority bond also known as PHAs - Public Housing Authority bonds, this is long-term debt used to finance the building of public housing. Like project notes, PHA bonds are backed by rents, U.S. Government subsidies, and the guarantee of the U.S. Government. These securities are no longer issued, but still trade in the secondary market.

New issue any security being offered and sold to the public in the primary market, with the proceeds of the offering going to the issuer. The issuance of the security may be an initial public offering (IPO) for a company that is "going public" for the first time; or a so-called secondary distribution, where an already public company is coming back to market with a subsequent securities offering.

New York Stock Exchange the auction trading market for the largest capitalization companies in the United States with a physical trading floor located in lower Manhattan.

No par stock stock that has no par value. Because some states tax a corporation on the par value of its stock, a corporation may choose to assign its stock a par value of zero in order to avoid the tax.

No-load fund   a mutual fund (i.e., open-end management company) that has no sales charge added into its public offering price. In a no-load fund, the net asset value (NAV) and the public offering price (POP) are the same. Today, a true no-load fund has no front-end load, no back-end load or contingent deferred sales charge, and no 12-b-1 fees. (compare Load fund)

Nominal quote   in the over-the-counter market, a dealer's approximation of a price of where the security may be trading. This is really no quote, since the dealer is not required to trade at this price. Nominal quotes are only found for non-NASDAQ issues. All NASDAQ quotes must be "firm." (compare Firm quote, Subject quote)

Nominal yield   also known as the coupon rate or stated yield, the fixed annual rate of interest (as a percentage of the bond's par value) paid to the purchaser of a bond. (see Coupon rate, Stated yield)

Non-accredited investor   a private placement investor under Regulation D who is not wealthy enough to be "accredited." A maximum of 35 non-accredited investors are permitted in a private placement for the transaction to be exempt under the Securities Act of 1933.

Non-callable security   a bond or preferred stock that cannot be redeemed early or repurchased by the issuer. Such a security would not contain call provisions in its trust indenture. Issuers will sell non-callable issues during periods when interest rates are low, since the issuer does not need the option to refinance the issue at a later date by calling in the issuer if interest rates should drop in the future - they are already as low as they are likely to be.

Non-competitive bid   a bid that can be placed by individuals and secondary dealers at the weekly Treasury auctions, this type of bid does not specify a bid yield. The non-competitive bids are reserved out of the auction and are filled at the average yield of the winning competitive bids. Thus, non-competitive bids are assured of being filled. (compare Competitive bid auction)

Non-convertible bond   a debt security that is not convertible into the common stock of the issuing company.

Non-cumulative preferred stock   rarely issued, preferred stock that does not accumulate any unpaid dividends that must all be paid before a common dividend can be paid. (compare Cumulative preferred stock)

Non-diversified fund   a definition under the Investment Company Act of 1940, a non-diversified fund is one that does not meet the "75/5/10" rule. To be diversified, a fund must have at least 75% of its assets invested in securities; with no more than 5% of these assets invested in any one company's securities; with no holding exceeding 10% of the voting stock of any one company. If these tests are not met, then the fund is "non-diversified." (compare Diversified fund)

Non-durable power of attorney   a power of attorney that ceases upon the mental incapacitation of the grantor (compare durable power of attorney).

Non-exempt security   a security which is not exempt from the provisions of the Securities Act of 1933 and the Securities and Exchange Act of 1934. Essentially, corporate securities are non-exempt. Government issues, agency issues, municipal issues, among others, are all exempt securities.

Non-managed fee based account   a brokerage account where a flat annual fee is imposed for all trades performed in a year. Note that this type of account does not include investment management or portfolio allocation services, and thus is not considered to be an advisory product. (compare Wrap account)

Non-managed offering   the underwriting of a limited partnership in which the issuer, known as the syndicator, forms and registers the partnership, and then offers it directly to brokerage firms for sale to the public through its own employees, known as wholesalers. (see Syndicator, Wholesaler; compare Managed offering)

Non-negotiable security   a security which cannot be traded; i.e., a redeemable security. For example, common stock is negotiable and trades in the public markets; whereas mutual fund shares are redeemable with the sponsor - they do not trade.

Non-recourse loan in a limited partnership, loans to the partnership for which the limited partner is not personally liable. If the partnership fails, the lender cannot make a claim against each limited partner personally for the unpaid loan amount. Since the limited partner is not "at risk" for non-recourse loans, these are excluded from the limited partner's tax basis - with the exception of real estate mortgage non-recourse financing. (compare Recourse loan)

Non-self supporting debt municipal general obligation bonds that are paid from tax collections; they are not paid from the revenues from a facility. General obligation bonds are non-self supporting debts since they are "carried on the backs of the taxpayers." Revenue bonds are self-supporting debts, since the revenues from the facility pay for the running of the facility - there is no burden on taxpayers. (compare Self supporting debt)

Non-systematic risk the risk component of a portfolio that can be diversified away. As more and more stocks are added to the portfolio, the portfolio becomes the "market" and is left only with systematic, or market, risk. (see Systematic risk)

Non-tax qualified plan a pension or retirement plan in which the contributions are not deductible against the contributor's taxable income. In effect, the contribution is made with after-tax dollars. All earnings on the contributions are still tax-deferred; however, when distributions begin, only the tax-deferred earnings build-up is taxed. (compare Non-tax qualified plan)

Non-voting stock common stock that does not have the right to vote. This type of security is sometimes issued in order to avoid a hostile takeover.

Normal yield curve a graph of the yields of fixed income securities of the same type (e.g., U.S. Governments or Corporates or Municipals) by maturity. As the maturity lengthens, the yield increases, so the curve ascends. This is a "normal" yield curve shape, showing that investors will accept lower yields for shorter maturities; but demand higher yields for longer maturities (since there is greater risk). (compare Flat yield curve, Inverted yield curve)

Not held order a market order in which the investor gives the floor broker discretion as to the time and price at which the order will be executed. Such a market order is "not held" to an immediate execution, as is the case with a regular market order. Specialists are not permitted to accept "Not Held" orders. (see Floor broker)

Note a medium term security with a maturity of two to ten years. The term is commonly used to refer to U.S. Government securities with a maturity of two to ten years, known as Treasury Notes.

Numbered account an account used to maintain the anonymity of the investors. All order tickets and records for the customer show a number, instead of the customer's name. The firm must keep on file the customer's name and a statement verifying ownership of the account.

NYSE the abbreviation for the New York Stock Exchange.

NYSE Composite Index a weighted index that includes all of the common issues (approximately 3000) that trade on the New York Stock Exchange.

O

OCC abbreviation of the Options Clearing Corporation, a clearing organization owned by the exchanges that trade options. The OCC issues all listed option contracts; sets the standards for these contracts; handles exercises of the contracts; and guarantees the performance or obligation of the option seller under the terms of the contract.

Odd first interest payment a new issue bond whose first coupon payment will encompass less than six months of interest. Since most bonds pay interest on January 1st and July 1st (very easy to remember these dates!), if such a bond is issued, say in November, the first interest payment will occur on January 1st, covering 2 months of interest (November and December. Thereafter, the bond pays interest on the regular semi-annual January 1st and July 1st dates. This is also called a "short coupon bond."

Odd lot theory an amusing technical theory that states that small investors trade odd lots and small investors are wrong. Therefore, if the small investor is buying, one should sell; if the small investor is selling, one should buy.

Odd lot trade a stock trade involving less than 100 shares. On the NYSE, the Specialist acts as the odd lot dealer. (compare Round lot)

OEX the symbol for stock index options traded on the Standard and Poor's 100 index. The term OEX comes from "Options Exchange Index" because this was the very first index option introduced (by the CBOE).

Offer synonym for the "ask" price.

Offering circular another name for the disclosure document for a new issue that is exempt from the registration and prospectus requirements of the Securities Act of 1933. More specifically, Offering Circulars are used in offerings made under a Regulation A exemption. (see Regulation A)

Offering memorandum   also called a Private Placement memorandum, the disclosure document used in connection with a Regulation D private placement offering. Because this transaction is exempt, no prospectus is required under the Securities Act of 1933. (see Regulation D)

Offers wanted   abbreviated by "OW" in dealer listings such as the OTCBB, Pink Sheets, or Yellow Sheets, this shows that the dealer wants to buy a specific security that he does not see offered currently, and is soliciting offers of the security from potential sellers. (compare Bids Wanted)

Office of the Comptroller of Currency   abbreviated OCC, this part of the Department of Treasury inspects and audits commercial banks for compliance with Federal banking laws.

Office of Thrift Supervision   abbreviated OTS, this part of the Department of Treasury inspects and audits savings and loans for compliance with Federal banking laws.

Official notice of sale   an advertisement published by a municipality in The Bond Buyer and local newspapers, that solicits competitive bids from investment banks and commercial banks that may want to underwrite a proposed new issue.

The advertisement details the terms of the proposed bond issue, which the potential underwriter must consider when formulating its bid. These terms include the type of bonds that will be issued, the total dollar amount of the issue, the type of security backing the bond, the reputation of the bond counsel for the issue, the amount of the good faith deposit, and the last day to submit bids (among many other items).

Official statement the disclosure document for a new municipal bond offering which details the material information necessary for the investor to judge the creditworthiness of an issue and to determine whether or not to invest. Note that there is no prospectus requirement for municipals because they are exempt issues under the Securities Act of 1933. The MSRB does not regulate municipal issuers, so it cannot force municipal issuers to provide an Official Statement. However, municipal underwriters are obligated to obtain a copy of the Official Statement and perform due diligence on it prior to engaging in a municipal underwriting; and if an Official Statement has been prepared (which it will be because of the due diligence requirement), then the MSRB obligates the underwriter to give it to purchasers no later than settlement. (see Exempt securities)

Omnibus account an account established with a broker-dealer by an investment adviser and used to make trades for his or her customers. The broker-dealer firm essentially serves as a back office for the investment adviser - accepting checks from customers, sending out confirmations and monthly statements, and keeping account records.

OPD an abbreviation appearing next to a stock's symbol on the ticker indicating that the opening of trading in a stock is delayed.

Open interest a term associated with the options markets which is the total amount of long or short positions standing open in the market. As investors open new positions, open interest increases . As investors liquidate (close) their positions; or as contracts expire; open interest decreases.

Open market operations the buying and selling of U.S. Government securities, and other eligible securities, in the open market by the Federal Reserve. Managed by the Federal Open Market Committee (FOMC), open market operations are a tool of monetary policy that is used every day. The Fed will sell eligible securities to member banks (draining the banks of cash) to tighten the money supply; and will buy eligible securities from member banks (injecting cash into the banks) to loosen the money supply. (see Eligible securities)

135

Open order   same as a good-til-canceled (GTC) order, these are orders placed "away from the current market" that are to be executed if the market moves to, or through, that price. Thus, these are limit, stop, and stop-limit orders. GTC orders remain open in the market until they are either executed or canceled. (see Stop order, Limit order, Stop-limit order)

Open repo   a repurchase agreement with no specific date to buy back the securities. The agreement remains open on a day-to-day basis and may be terminated by either party at any time. (see Repurchase agreement)

Open-end fund   known commonly as a "mutual fund," an open-end management company is a type of investment company that establishes a diversified portfolio of investments and then continually issues new shares and redeems its own shares representing ownership in the portfolio. Mutual fund shares are redeemable securities with the sponsor; they are non-negotiable and do not trade (see Mutual fund; compare Closed-end fund)

Open-end management company   known commonly as a "mutual fund," an open-end management company is a type of investment company that establishes a diversified portfolio of investments and then continually issues new shares and redeems its own shares representing ownership in the portfolio. Mutual fund shares are redeemable securities with the sponsor; they are non-negotiable and do not trade. (see Mutual fund; compare Closed-end management company)

Open-end mortgage bond   a provision in a mortgage bond's trust indenture that allows a corporation to issue additional bonds backed by the same real estate that has been pledged as collateral for existing bonds. The issuance of such bonds, which have equal status to the already outstanding bonds backed by the same real estate, is contingent upon the property value increasing, so that there is always an excess of property value backing all of the outstanding mortgage bonds. (see Mortgage bond; compare Closed-end mortgage bond)

Opening purchase   in the options market, when an investor's initial option transaction in a specific contract is a purchase (i.e., the investor becomes the holder of) a call or put option. Such a position is terminated with a closing sale. (see Closing sale; compare Opening sale, Closing purchase)

Opening sale   in the options market, when an investor's initial option transaction in a specific contract is a sale (i.e., the investor becomes the writer of) a call or put option. Such a position is terminated with a closing purchase. (see Closing purchase; compare Opening purchase; Closing sale)

Operations and maintenance fund   a separate account established under the "flow of funds" provisions of a municipal revenue bond trust indenture, to receive required annual payments made by the issuer to pay for operation and maintenance of a facility built with the proceeds of a revenue bond issue. (see Flow of funds)

Option   a contract that gives the holder the right to either buy or sell securities at a specified price (the strike or exercise price) for a specified period of time. The writer of the option contract is either obligated to sell or buy when the holder exercises the contract. The two types of options are call options and put options. There are option contracts on stocks, debt securities, foreign currencies, and stock indexes. (see Call option, Put option)

Option class   all calls on a single issuer are one class of options; and all puts on that issuer are another class of options. For example, all IBM calls are a "class;" and all IBM puts are a "class."

Optional call   a call provision in a bond contract that gives the issuer the option of calling in the bonds at predetermined dates and prices, if the issuer wishes to do so. Such a provision would be used by the issuer if interest rates dropped substantially after issuance of the bonds. (compare Mandatory call)

Options agreement   an agreement drawn up after a customer is approved for options trading that reconfirms the suitability information given by the customer; and which states the types and levels of options transactions that the customer can perform in the account based upon that suitability determination. It also states that the customer agrees to abide by the rules and regulations of the OCC. The customer must sign and return the options agreement no later than 15 days after the account is opened. (compare Options disclosure document)

Options Clearing Corporation   the clearing organization owned all of the exchanges that trade options, the OCC issues all listed option contracts, standardizes these contracts; handles exercises of the contracts; and guarantees the performance or obligation of the option seller under the terms of the contract. (see OCC)

Options Clearing Corporation prospectus   an extremely detailed disclosure document that is available to options customers upon request, the OCC Prospectus details all of the rules and procedures of the Options Clearing Corporation that affect options customers.

Options Disclosure Document   published by the Options Clearing Corporation, a document that explains the basic risks, uses, and important rules of options investing. It is required that a broker-dealer to send the Options Disclosure Document to the customer, at or before, the opening of an options account. (compare Options agreement)

Order   a memorandum of a customer's specific instructions regarding buying or selling securities on his or her behalf.

Order Book Official   called an OBO, an options exchange employee who maintains the book of public customers' options orders that are placed away from the market. Like a board broker, an OBO acts only as an agent in options transactions. OBOs are appointed by the exchange to handle the book for less actively traded options contracts. (compare Board broker)

Order department   part of a brokerage firm's operations or "back office" that is responsible for routing buy and sell orders to the proper markets (exchanges or OTC) for execution and confirming the execution of those orders for the firm and its customers.

Order period   in a competitive bid underwriting of a new issue municipal bond, a short period of time following the award of the issue to the winning underwriter. Once the bid is won, all Pre-sale orders are filled. If bonds remain unsold in the syndicate account, the manager establishes an order period (typically 1/2 hour) during which all syndicate members are expected to contact customers who previously expressed interest but who did not place an order. These orders collected during the order period are known as Group net orders, since they benefit the syndicate group. (see Pre-sale order, Group order, Priority provisions)

Order Support System   abbreviated "OSS," this is the CBOE's automated options trading system. (see OSS)

Order ticket   the form on which a broker records the specific details of a customer's buy or sell order.

Original issue discount   a bond issued with a below market rate of interest, so that the issue price is below par. The "missing" interest income (that amount below the market rate) constitutes the discount on the bond. The IRS views the discount as interest income that must be accreted over the life of the bond. (compare Original issue premium)

Original issue premium   a bond issued with an above market rate of interest, so that the issue price is above par. The "extra" interest income (that amount above the market rate) constitutes the premium on the bond. The IRS views the premium paid as a loss that is a reduction of annual interest income to be amortized over the life of the bond. (compare Original issue discount)

OSS   abbreviation for Order Support System, the automated options trading system used at the Chicago Board Options Exchange (CBOE).

OTC   common abbreviation of the over-the-counter market. (see Second market)

OTC Bulletin Board (OTCBB)   an electronic system that disseminates real-time quotes for smaller OTC non-NASDAQ stocks. The OTC Bulletin Board (OTCBB), also known as the Electronic Bulletin Board, will eventually replace the Pink Sheets. (see NASDAQ, Pink sheets, Electronic bulletin board)

OTC margin stock   any stock trading in the over-the-counter market that can be bought on margin under Regulation T. All NASDAQ stocks and OTC stocks on the Federal Reserve Board's margin list are OTC margin stocks. Note that "Pink Sheet" non-NASDAQ stocks are generally not marginable. (see Pink sheets)

Out of the money   in option trading, a phrase that describes an option that has no intrinsic value. Specifically, an option is "out-of-the-money" when the relationship between the market price of the underlying security and the option's strike price is such that the holder (buyer) will not exercise the option because to do so would result in a loss. A call (or a warrant) is "out the money" when the market price of the underlying stock is lower than the call's strike price or warrant's exercise price. A put is "out the money" when the market price of the underlying stock is higher than the put's strike price. (compare At the money, In the money)

Outstanding stock   the number of shares that have been issued that are actually outstanding in the hands of the public. Corporate repurchases of Treasury Stock are deducted from issued stock to find the number of shares outstanding.

Over-the-counter (OTC) market   a decentralized, negotiated market in which many dealers in diverse locations execute trades for customers over an electronic trading system such as NASDAQ or over telephone lines.

Overbought market usually interpreted as an indicator of a future price decline, a technical term used to describe a stock (or market) whose value has risen quickly and unexpectedly, far above its actual worth. Such an overpriced stock (or market) is ripe for a decline. (compare Oversold market)

Overlapping debt debt that a municipal issuer such as a city or township shares with another legal issuer which overlaps the geographical boundaries of that city or township. Examples of such overlapping debts are bonds issued by counties and districts, such as school districts or road districts.

Overnight repo a repurchase agreement in which the selling party agrees to repurchase the securities the next day. This is the most common duration of a repurchase agreement. (see Repurchase agreement)

Overriding royalty interest a sharing arrangement in an oil and gas partnership where the general partner bears none of the costs; and the limited partners bear all the costs. From the first barrel of oil produced, the general partner and limited partners split the oil revenues. (compare Disproportionate sharing arrangement, Net profits interest, Reversionary working interest)

Oversold market usually interpreted as an indication of an impending price rise, a technical term to describe a stock (or the market) whose value has fallen quickly and sharply, far below its actual worth. Such a stock (or market) is ripe for a turnaround. (compare Overbought market)

OW abbreviation for Offers Wanted, in dealer listings such as the OTCBB, Pink Sheets, or Yellow Sheets, this shows that the dealer wants to buy a specific security that he does not see offered currently, and is soliciting offers of the security from potential sellers. (compare BW - Bids Wanted.)

_P_

P/E ratio   acronym for the Price / Earnings ratio, this is a stock's current market price divided by its annual earnings. It is a measure of the number of times that a stock's price exceeds its earnings - in short, how expensive the stock is relative to its earnings. This is sometimes called the "multiple" - for example, if a stock is selling at a multiple of 20, and the company has earnings of $2.50 per share, then the stock is trading at $50 per share (20 x $2.50).

PAC tranch   a PAC, or Planned Amortization Class Tranch, is buffered by surrounding companion tranches that absorb prepayment and extension risk before these risks affect the PAC tranch. This tranch has the most certain repayment date. (see Tranch, Prepayment risk, Extension risk; compare Companion tranch, Targeted Amortization Class).

Par   1) for common stock, an arbitrary (and essentially meaningless) value assigned the shares at the time of issuance; 2) for preferred stock, a share's fixed value upon which dividend payments are based - usually $50 par or $100 par; 3) for a bond, the fixed value (usually $1,000) upon which interest payments are based. Par value and face value are synonyms when applied to bonds.

Par bond   a bond whose current secondary market price is equal to its principal or face value. This bond is neither trading at a discount; nor at a premium; to par.

Par value   1) for common stock, an arbitrary (and essentially meaningless) value assigned the shares at the time of issuance; 2) for preferred stock, a share's fixed value upon which dividend payments are based - usually $50 par or $100 par; 3) for a bond, the fixed value (usually $1,000) upon which interest payments are based. Par value and face value are synonyms when applied to bonds.

Parity   1) for convertible bonds and convertible preferred stock, when the total market value of the common shares into which a security can be converted equals the market value of the convertible security; 2) for options, when the premium of the option is exactly equal to the option's intrinsic value. (see Intrinsic value)

Participating preferred stock   the preferred shareholder receives the fixed dividend and also participates in better than expected earnings with the common shareholder. This "extra" dividend is payable to both the preferred and common stock only if the earnings for common exceed a specified amount. These securities are rarely issued today.

Participating UIT   a unit investment trust that invests in the shares of mutual funds, this is the typical investment company form for variable annuity separate accounts.

Participation certificates (PCs)   the name for the pass-through certificates issued by the Federal Home Loan Mortgage Corp., a "privatized" federal agency that is now a for-profit company whose common stock is listed on the NYSE. (see Pass-through certificate, Federal Home Loan Mortgage Corp.)

Partnership account   a securities account opened by a partnership. Before the account can be opened, a copy of the partnership agreement must be submitted to the broker-dealer.

Partnership agreement   in a direct participation program or limited partnership, the document that details the rights and obligations of both the general partner and the limited partner.

Partnership democracy   the right of limited partners to: 1) vote on partnership matters, including the admission of a new general partner to the limited partnership, or the sale of the partnership's assets; 2) sue the general partner; 3; receive the remaining assets in a liquidation of the partnership; 4) inspect the books and records of the partnership.

Pass-through certificate a security representing the holder's participation in a pool of securities, e.g., mortgages, etc. Payments from the underlying securities are "passed-through" to the certificate holders. The payments that the security holder receives consist of both interest and principal, just like a mortgage payment. Under current IRS rules, the interest portion is fully taxable.

Passive asset management the pursuit of investment returns to match, but not exceed, the specific benchmark return. Passive asset managers believe that undervalued stocks do not exist in the marketplace, and that they can only match the performance of a similar index fund. (compare Active asset management)

Passive income (losses) a definition under the tax code, this is income (or losses) realized from investments in real estate or limited partnership investments. Passive losses can only be offset against other passive income; they cannot be offset against earned income or portfolio income. (compare Earned income, Portfolio income)

Passive return the return achieved by an asset manager to match the specified benchmark (compare Active return)

Pattern day trader any person who executes 4 or more day trades in a 5 business day period. Pattern day traders are subject to stricter suitability standards and higher minimum margins.

Payable date the date, set by the issuer, on which a cash dividend will be paid; or a stock or rights distribution will be made; to an investor who has purchased the stock before the appropriate ex date. If the security is purchased before the ex date, the purchaser will show as an owner of record to receive the distribution from the issuer. The Payable date is typically 2 weeks after the Record date. (see Ex date, Record date)

Paying agent also called a disbursing agent, usually a commercial bank or trust company that receives funds from the issuer of a security and is then responsible for distributing dividends to stockholders and interest and principal payments to bondholders.

Payment for order flow a payment to retail member firms made by a market maker for routing their orders to that specific market maker. This practice is permitted, as long as the market maker's execution price is the "best available" at that time.

Payroll deduction savings plan more commonly called a 401(k) plan, a corporate pension plan to which an employee contributes a percentage of his or her salary via payroll deduction. These contributions are made with pre-tax dollars. In some cases, the employer will match each employee's contribution to the plan up to a certain percentage. A 401(k) plan with this feature is sometimes called a matching plan.

Penalty bid clause a clause in the syndicate agreement for anew issue underwriting designed to prevent syndicate members from selling a sticky issue back to the managing underwriter. If a syndicate member sells too many shares back to the lead underwriter by "hitting the stabilizing bid," the lead underwriter will repurchase them at the bid price, but will penalize the member by deducting any underwriter's concession that the member would have received. (see Stabilization, Sticky issue)

Penny stock low-priced, extremely speculative OTC stock issued by a small, start-up company with no earnings history. Any stock that is not exchange or NASDAQ listed, with a value of less, than $5, is considered a penny stock. If such stocks are recommended, a detailed suitability determination must be completed by the broker, and signed by the customer, prior to confirmation.

Penny stock rule SEC Rules 15-g-1 through 15-g-6, a set of SEC rules that have been adopted by the NASD (now FINRA) requiring that any customers who are solicited to buy a non-exchange, non-NASDAQ stock under $5, sign a detailed suitability statement that prominently discloses the high risks involved with such a security, prior to confirmation of sale.

Percentage depletion an annual non-cash expense deducted for the "using up" of natural resources (e.g., oil, gas, timber) owned by a business. In a direct participation program (DPP), the depletion allowance enables the business to recover the cost of buying the natural resource. The depletion allowance can be computed on a cost or percentage basis. Under percentage depletion, the business deducts a percentage (set by Congress) of the price at which the natural resource is sold, regardless of its actual cost. (compare Cost depletion)

Percentage of par value   a price quote for a bond that is a percentage of the bond's face value. The prices of corporate, U.S. Government, and Agency bonds are always quoted as a percentage of par value. On the other hand, most municipal bonds are quoted on a yield basis. (see Basis quote)

Performance preferred   a not-widely used name for preferred stock· issued by a growth company. Also, another name for participating preferred stock.

Performance stock   another name for growth stocks. These are securities that the investor expects will show quick capital appreciation. (see Growth stock)

Perpetual warrant   usually attached to a new bond or preferred stock issue as a "sweetener" to increase the issue's marketability. a warrant gives the holder the right to buy a stated amount of common stock at a specified price. This specified price is initially higher than the stock's current market price. For the warrant to have value, the market price of the stock must rise above the exercise price of the warrant. Currently issued warrants have a limited life; however, in the past, some companies have issued "perpetual" warrants that have no expiration date. Warrants trade separately in the market.

PHA bond   acronym for Public Housing Authority bond, this is long-term debt used to finance the building of public housing. Like project notes, PHA bonds are backed by rents, U.S. Government subsidies, and the guarantee of the U.S. Government. These securities are no longer issued, but still trade in the secondary market.

Phantom income   if a business abandons a piece of property or machinery against which there is a loan, and the lender repossesses the asset, if the unpaid loan amount exceeds the balance due, and this amount is "forgiven" by the lender, then this amount is "phantom income" to the investor, and is taxable. Essentially, the standpoint of the IRS is that relief of a liability is "income" to the taxpayer.

Philadelphia Stock Exchange   a regional stock exchange that trades stocks, listed options, and foreign currency options. This was the very first stock exchange in the United States, and is known as the "PHLX." In late 2007, NASDAQ purchased the PHLX, mainly for its options trading business.

PHLX   the abbreviation for the Philadelphia Stock Exchange, a regional stock exchange that trades stocks, options, and foreign currency options.

Pink sheets   named for the color of the paper and published weekly by the National Quotations Bureau, a listing of the bid and ask prices of certain thinly traded OTC stocks - mostly low-priced and foreign issues that are too small to be included on the NASDAQ system.

Placement ratio   published on "The Numbers Page" at the back of The Bond Buyer, the portion of the total dollar amount of new issue bonds purchased by underwriters from issuers; that have been subsequently resold to the public. The ratio shows how well the marketplace is absorbing new issues. (see Bond buyer)

Plain vanilla CMO tranch   the simplest form of CMO tranch structure, a plain vanilla CMO divides the underlying mortgage cash flows sequentially into a fixed number of tranches, creating a number of expected maturities. (see Tranch; compare PAC tranch, TAC tranch, Companion tranch)

Plan completion insurance   normally refers to the waiver of premium provision, it states if a customer is unable to contribute the payments to a variable annuity contract due to death, then the insurance company will complete the contractual agreement by making a lump sum payment to the plan custodian.

Planned amortization class   a PAC, or Planned Amortization Class Tranch, is buffered by surrounding companion tranches that absorb prepayment and extension risk before these risks affect the PAC tranch. This tranch has the most certain repayment date. (see Tranch, Prepayment risk, Extension risk; compare Companion tranch, Targeted Amortization Class).

Point   1) for common and preferred stock, the price movement on an individual stock equal to $1; 2) for bonds, the price movement equal to 1% of $1,000 par value, which is $10.

Poison pill   jargon used to describe a security whose features are specifically designed to defend against a hostile takeover.

Political risk   the risk of actions of a foreign government affecting that country's debt instruments and currency value.

POP   acronym for Public Offering Price, this is: 1) for stocks and bonds, the price at which new shares are sold to the public by their issuer or underwriters. Bonds and preferred stock are usually issued at par value. The "POP" includes the underwriter's spread; 2) for mutual funds, the ask price at which an investor purchases a mutual fund share. Again, the "POP" includes any sales charge imposed by the fund.

Portfolio income   a definition under the tax code, this is dividends, interest, and capital gains (or capital losses) realized on investments in securities. (compare Earned income, Passive income)

Portfolio margin   introduced in mid-2007, a "risk-based" method of computing margin requirements that can result in lower margins and greater leverage than the "strategy based" margins of Regulation T. Portfolio margin is only permitted for institutional and wealthy investors.

Portfolio rebalancing   the reallocation of funds in an asset allocation model from overperforming asset classes to those that have underperformed. In this manner, the percentage allocations to each asset class are kept within the desired range.

Position limit   under Options Clearing Corporation (OCC) regulation, the maximum number of options positions that an investor can maintain on the same "side" of the market on the same underlying security. Long calls and short puts are the same side of the market because in both cases the investor is bullish and will buy securities if and when the option is exercised. Long puts and short calls are the same side of the market because in both cases the investor is bearish and will sell securities if and when the option is exercised. (see: Sides of the market)

Position trading   buying a security into; or selling a security out of; a broker-dealer's own inventory. When a firm "position trades," it is trading for its own account; as opposed to executing a transaction for a customer. (see Market maker)

Pre-refunding   when interest rates have dropped, a municipal issuer who has sold bonds that are callable can issue a new municipal bond with a lower coupon rate and use the proceeds to buy other bonds (usually U.S. Government securities) which are placed in escrow. The income from the U.S. Governments pays the interest on the older high rate outstanding municipal debt and when the Governments mature, the proceeds are used to retire the old, outstanding municipal issue on their first call date. In effect, the issuer is prepaying both interest and principal on the old bonds with the U.S. Government securities which are held in trust. Both the new bond and the pre-refunded old bond are both outstanding at the same time, until the first in-whole call date, when the pre-refunded bond is called in with the proceeds of the maturing escrowed Government securities. (see Advanced refunding, Defeasance)

Pre-sale order   in a competitive bid underwriting of a new issue municipal bond, an order (more accurately an indication of intention to buy) that the underwriter solicits before the municipality announces the winning bid. The collection of the Pre-Sale orders aids the underwriter in determining the interest rates to bid. Pre-sale orders are filled only if the underwriter wins the bid. These are the first orders to be filled in new issue municipal bond offering. (see Priority provisions, Order period)

Preemptive right   an entitlement that enables common stockholders to maintain proportionate ownership in a company when the company issues new shares. If a company wishes to issue additional common shares, its gives its existing shareholders rights certificates to buy the new shares, at a discount from the current market price. An existing stockholder can use the rights to subscribe to the new shares or may sell the rights to someone else. These rights usually expire in thirty days. (see Subscription right)

Preferred stock   an equity security that is senior to common stock. It pays a fixed dividend rate and usually has no voting or preemptive rights. It has preference over common shares as to dividend distributions and in a liquidation, hence it is a "senior" security.

Preferred stock fund   a management company that invests in high dividend paying preferred stocks. these are designed for investment by corporations with excess funds to invest, so they can take advantage of the 70% corporate dividend exclusion from taxation.

Preferred stock ratio   the ratio of a company's preferred stockholders' equity to total long term capital. Preferred stockholders' equity is the total value of preferred at par value. Total long term capital consists of common stockholders' equity, preferred stockholder's equity, and long term debt. Common stockholders' equity consists of common at par + capital in excess of par + retained earnings.

Preferred stockholder's equity   the portion of a company's long term capital raised from selling preferred stock (typically at par value) to shareholders.

Preliminary official statement   the red herring for a new municipal bond offering that is used by the underwriters to get an indication of the investor interest in the issue. Potential investors use this document to make a preliminary evaluation of the investment quality and credit worthiness of a new municipal bond issue. (see Red herring; compare Official statement)

Preliminary prospectus   also known as the "red herring" because of the disclaimer printed in red on the cover, this is the preliminary prospectus which may be sent to potential purchasers of a new non-exempt securities issue during the 20-day cooling off period under the Securities Act of 1933. Legally, the preliminary prospectus does not offer the securities, since this is prohibited during the cooling off period. The red herring is used to get an indication of the public's interest in a security before the final price is set and the security is issued. (see Cooling off period, Prospectus)

Premium   1) the amount by which the market value of a bond or preferred stock exceeds its par value; 2) the amount paid over par for a security (compare Discount); 3) the market price of a call option or a put option.

Premium bond   a bond whose market price is greater than its par value. Stated another way, a bond whose market value is in excess of its par value. (compare Discount bond)

Prepayment risk   associated with pass-through agency securities (FNMA, GNMA, FHLMC), and their derivatives such as CMOs - collateralized mortgage obligations, this is the risk that the homeowners whose mortgages back the certificates will repay the principal earlier than expected - in effect, retiring the bond before its expected maturity. This would occur if the homeowners can refinance their mortgages at lower current interest rates. (see CMO, Mortgage backed security, Pass-through security; compare Extension risk)

Price   in technical terms, this is the point at which supply (sellers) and demand (buyers) converge and a trade occurs.

Price spread   an option spread position, where simultaneously the same type of option is bought and sold with different strike prices; and the same expiration. When the positions are "stacked" one above the other, there is a difference in the strike prices, hence the name. These are also called "vertical" spreads. There are 4 types of price spreads - bull call spreads, bear call spreads, bull put spreads, and bear put spreads. (compare Time spread, Diagonal spread)

Price-earnings ratio   a ratio in which a stock's current market price is divided by its annual earnings. It is a measure of the number of times that a stock's price exceeds its earnings - in short, how expensive the stock is relative to its earnings. This is sometimes called the "multiple" - for example, if a stock is selling at a multiple of 20, and the company has earnings of $2.50 per share, then the stock is trading at $50 per share (20 x $2.50).

Primary dealer   a U.S. Government securities dealer that has been so designated by the Federal Reserve. Primary dealers can trade directly with the Fed and must participate in the weekly Treasury auctions. Commercial banks, foreign banks, and domestic and foreign broker-dealers are among the 20 or so designated primary dealers.

Primary issue   another name for a new issue security.

Primary market   the market in which the issuer first offers and sell its securities to the public, with proceeds from the sale going to the issuing corporation. (compare Secondary market)

Primary offering   the issuance of new securities by a company to the public under a prospectus as required under the Securities Act of 1933, unless an exemption from registration is available. The net proceeds from the offering go to the issuer. (compare Secondary offering)

Prime banker's acceptance   a banker's acceptance, issued by one of the top credit rated money center banks, that is eligible for trading with the Federal Reserve in the Fed's open market operations. (see Banker's acceptance, Open market operations)

Prime paper   investment grade commercial paper rated P3 or better. This is the highest grade of commercial paper, which is rated by Moody's as follows: P1 (highest quality), P2 (higher quality), and P3 (high quality). Anything below P3 is rated NP - and is "Not Prime."

Prime rate   the short-term interest rate that commercial banks charge their most credit-worthy business customers.

Principal transaction   a trade where a member firm acts as a dealer in the transaction, selling the security to the customer out of the firm's inventory; or buying the security into the firm's inventory from the customer. When effecting a principal transaction, the dealer earns a mark-up when the security is sold to a customer; and a mark-down when the security is bought from a customer. Also, a member firm can be a principal in an underwriting when it takes financial liability for the issue, as in a firm commitment underwriting. (compare Agency transaction)

Prior lien bond   a secured or unsecured bond that has priority over other outstanding bonds. The bonds are usually issued by companies trying to reorganize in order to avoid bankruptcy; and the existing bondholders will allow another bond issue to be sold that is "senior" to their position, in order for the company to get funds to continue to stay in business.

Prior preferred stock   sometimes called a senior preferred, preferred stock that has priority over other outstanding preferred issues in receiving dividend payments and making claims against the firm in a liquidation.

Priority provision   a provision in the syndicate letter that specifies the sequence in which orders for a new issue municipal bond offering will be filled by the manager. The MSRB requires that the manager disseminate this information to the syndicate. The usual sequence is: 1) Pre-sale orders; 2) Group net orders; 3) Designated orders; and 4) Member orders. (see Pre-sale order, Group net order, Designated order, Member order)

Private placement   an exempt transaction under Regulation D that can be sold without a prospectus to an unlimited number of accredited (wealthy) investors, but only to a maximum of thirty-five (35) non-accredited investors. In reality, private placements are sold to a relatively small number of institutional investors. (see Accredited investor)

Proceeds transaction   a trade in which the customer sells a security and uses the proceeds to buy another security. The two parts of this transaction are subject to two separate commissions or mark-ups. Under FINRA/NASD rules, the separate commissions or mark-ups are combined and the total charge is less than if two totally separate transactions had been performed. This is also known as a "dual agency" trade.

Production   the total proceeds that the municipal underwriting syndicate would receive if all of a new municipal bond offering were sold at the reoffering price. In other words, this is the dollar amount that the syndicate expects to "produce" when it sells the bonds to the public. (see Reoffering price, Spread)

Profit-sharing pension plan   a pension plan to which an employer makes contributions for each employee only when the company has profits. If the company is not profitable, then there are no mandatory contributions.

Progressive tax   a tax rate, such as that for personal income, that increases as one's income increases. (compare Regressive taxes)

Project note   a short-term municipal security used to start the building of a public housing project. The notes are redeemed from the proceeds of long-term bonds issued to finance the project over a much longer time frame. Project notes are backed by rents, U.S. Government subsidies, and the guarantee of the U.S. Government. These securities are no longer issued.

Proprietary something that belongs to the member firm or that is only sold by the member firm - for example, a member firm can have a proprietary mutual fund, meaning it is only sold by that firm and no one else.

Prospectus   a printed summary of the Securities and Exchange Commission-filed registration statement required for non-exempt securities offerings under the Securities Act of 1933 that discloses the details of a particular offering of securities, including the company's business history and that of its management; its future business plans; and its intended use of the proceeds from the issue. The prospectus must contain enough material information for the investor to be able to judge the merits of the issue, and must not omit any material information needed by the investor to make an informed decision. (see Registration statement)

Proxy   a form on which an investor votes his shares without physically being present at the stockholders' meeting by transferring his or her voting authority to another party.

Proxy department   part of a brokerage firm's operations or "back office" that is responsible for sending proxies to customers who hold securities in margin accounts. Since these securities are held in "street name," the issuer does not know the names of the owners of the shares - only the broker-dealer shows as the owner. The proxy department receives the proxy (voting) materials from the issuer and distributes them to the beneficial owners of the shares. (see Proxy, Street name)

Prudent man rule   under state law, a standard by which fiduciaries are expected to handle accounts over which they have control. Specifically, the law requires that the fiduciary handle the account and make investment decisions in the same way any prudent, intelligent person would, with emphasis on preservation of capital, a reasonable rate of return, and low risk. (see Fiduciary)

PSA   abbreviation for "Prepayment Speed Assumption" - which is the assumed rate of principal prepayment on the mortgages underlying a mortgage backed pass-through certificate. Also the abbreviation for Public Securities Association.

Public Housing Authority (PHA) bond   long-term debt used to finance the building of public housing. Like project notes, PHA bonds are backed by rents, U.S. Government subsidies, and the guarantee of the U.S. Government. These securities are no longer issued, but still trade in the secondary market.

Public offering price   1) for stocks and bonds, the price at which new shares are sold to the public by their issuer or underwriters. Bonds and preferred stock are usually issued at par value. The "POP" includes the underwriter's spread; 2) for mutual funds, the ask price at which an investor purchases a mutual fund share. Again, the "POP" includes any sales charge imposed by the fund.

Public Securities Association (PSA) a national trade group consisting of about 200 members that represents the interests of government and municipal bond dealers. It promotes the positions of the bond dealers on market and regulatory issues, as both an educational and lobbying institution. The trade group has been expanded to include corporate bond dealers and renamed the Bond Market Association (BMA), and in 2006, it merged with the SIA (Securities Industry Association) to form "SIFMA" - the Securities Industry and Financial Markets Association.

Publicly traded fund a closed-end management company, commonly known as a publicly-traded, or exchange-traded fund, this type of investment company issues a fixed number of negotiable shares to the public. These shares are not redeemable by the fund. Closed-end fund structures are used to invest in illiquid markets or securities, such as emerging markets funds and municipal bond funds. In an open-end (mutual fund), redemption requests can force the fund to sell securities from the portfolio. In a closed-end fund, there is no redemption, so there is no forced sale of illiquid investments due to a high amount of redemptions.

Closed-end funds trade in the secondary markets - exchange and OTC - like any other stock and are purchased through a broker-dealer. The shares' market price may be at, above, or below the shares' net asset value. (see Publicly traded fund, Closed-end management company; compare Open-end fund)

Purchase and Sales (P&S) department part of a brokerage firm's operations or "back office" that is responsible for processing and reconciling executed orders. The P&S department records order executions, computes monies due or payable, sends out confirmations to customers, and compares trades with contra-brokers.

Purchasing power risk also called inflation risk, this is the risk that inflation will erode the value of the money earned from investments. Purchasing power risk is most acute for long term bonds. If inflation rates rise, then market interest rates rise. And if market interest rates rise, bond prices fall, with long term bond prices falling the fastest.

Put/Call ratio the ratio of put option trades to call option trades on a given day. The ratio is a technical indicator of market sentiment. If the ratio is very high, it indicates that the market is oversold and is likely to go higher; conversely if the ratio is very low, it indicates that the market is overbought and is likely to go lower. (see Overbought market, Oversold market)

Put date the first date (and after) that the holder of a bond with a put feature can "put" the bond back to the issuer. Bonds with put options are rarely issued. If they are, the put option is at par.

Put feature a provision of a bond contract or preferred stock contract that permits the holder to "put" (sell) the securities back to the issuer at a pre-established price (usually par) prior to maturity. Holders will "put" the securities back to the issuer if interest rates have risen after issuance, allowing the holder to reinvest at higher current rates. (compare Call feature)

Put option a contract that gives the holder the right, but not the obligation, to sell a fixed amount of securities (e.g., 100 shares of stock) at the specified price (the strike or exercise price) for a fixed period of time. Thus, the holder can "put" or sell the security, at a fixed price. The holder pays the premium (the market price of the contract) for this privilege. The writer of the put contract is obligated to buy a fixed amount of securities at the strike price if the holder exercises. For granting this privilege, the writer of a put option receives the premium. (compare Call option)

Puttable bond a bond that can be redeemed at face value by the holder at a specific times before maturity. An investor will typically use this put feature when interest rates are rising, allowing the holder to receive the par value of the bond, which can be reinvested by the holder at higher current rates. (compare Callable bond)

Q

QIB acronym for a "Qualified Institutional Buyer" as defined under Rule 144A. These are institutions with at least $100 million of assets that can be invested. Such "QIBs" can buy unregistered private placement blocks and trade them with other "QIBs."

QQQQ the symbol for the NASDAQ 100 Exchange Traded Fund (ETF), an index fund traded on NASDAQ. The NASDAQ 100 ETF is commonly referred to as the "Qube."

QT slang abbreviation for questionable trades, it is what DKs are called at the New York Stock Exchange. (see DK)

Qualified institutional buyer defined under Rule 144A, an institution with at least $100 million of assets that can be invested. Such "QIBs" can buy unregistered private placement blocks and trade them with other "QIBs."

Qualified legal opinion sometimes called a conditional legal opinion, the written opinion of the bond counsel that contingencies exist which could affect the legality, validity, or tax-exempt status of a new issue municipal bond. (see Bond counsel; compare Unqualified legal opinion)

Qubes the common name for the NASDAQ 100 Exchange Traded Fund (ETF), an index fund traded on NASDAQ.

Quick ratio a stringent measure of a company's liquidity that excludes inventory and prepaid expenses from the company's current assets and takes the ratio of these "quick assets" (as in quickly convertible into cash) to total current liabilities. (see Current asset, Current liability)

R

Random walk theory contrary to both technical and fundamental analysis, the theory asserts that stock prices do not move in predictable patterns in response to information in the market; therefore, an investor who chooses stocks at random has an equal opportunity to make money as one who does elaborate analysis. In essence, the random walk theory argues that buying an index fund is the best way to invest - since, under this theory, over a long time frame, an investor can only do as well as the "market."

Rate covenant a promise by a revenue bond issuer, made in connection with a net revenue pledge, to keep increasing charges (a pledge to increase rates) for the use of the facility as operation and maintenance costs increase. (see Net revenue pledge)

Rating services independent companies that rate the risk of default and the quality of the cash flow or assets backing fixed income issues - bonds, preferred stocks, and commercial paper. The three rating agencies include (from largest to smallest) Moody's Investors Service, Standard and Poor's, and Fitch's.

Ratio spread an option spread in which the number of calls (or puts) bought and sold simultaneously are different. (see Spread)

Ratio write the sale of more than one call against a long stock position; or the sale of more than one put against a short stock position; to generate extra premium income in a stable market. For example, selling 2 calls against 100 shares of stock is a 2:1 ratio write.

Real estate investment trust (REIT) regulated as a closed-end management company, REITs purchase different kinds of real estate investments such as buildings, mortgages, and short-term construction loans. REITs can invest in property (Equity REIT) or can buy mortgages and other real estate loans (Mortgage REIT). This security trades on the exchanges or in the OTC market.

Real estate limited partnership (RELP)   known as a "RELP," this is a limited partnership that invests in real estate for the economic merit of the investment, coupled with the flow through of depreciation losses and other tax deductions and benefits to the partners.

Real estate mortgage investment conduit (REMIC)   essentially the same as a collateralized mortgage obligation (CMO, a REMIC provides an issuer with greater flexibility in grouping the underlying mortgages into many different classes, including maturity and risk, and thereby creating more tranches. (see CMO, tranch)

Real interest rate   the yield to maturity of a long term bond reduced by the inflation rate. This is the "real" rate of return earned on the bond, after factoring out the effects of inflation.

Realized gain   the cash profit resulting from the liquidation of a security position.

Reallowance   a small portion of the underwriting spread which the managing underwriter allocates to a non-syndicate, non-selling group broker-dealer who sells part of a new issue.

Recapture   the reclaiming of a tax benefit previously taken when as asset is sold under IRS rules. For example, when a limited partnership sells a piece of machinery on which depreciation deductions were taken, any capital gain on the sale, to the extent of depreciation taken, is taxed at higher ordinary income tax rates (not the lower long term capital gains tax rate).

Recession   a decline in Gross Domestic Product (or Gross National Product) for two consecutive quarters. (compare Depression)

Reclamation   if a delivery of securities from one dealer to another is accepted, and later discovered not to be "good," then the accepting dealer can return the securities under his right of reclamation for correction of the problem. (compare Rejection)

Record date   the deadline date, set by a corporation's Board of Directors, on which an investor must be recorded as an owner of the stock in order to be eligible to receive a corporate distribution such as a cash dividend, stock dividend, stock split or rights. Note that holders of securities are "recorded" as of settlement date, not trade date. (compare Declaration date, Ex date)

Recourse loan   in a limited partnership, loans to the partnership for which the limited partner is personally liable. If the partnership fails, the lender can make a claim against each limited partner personally for the unpaid loan amount. Since the limited partner is "at risk" for recourse loans, these are included in the limited partner's tax basis. (compare Non-recourse loan)

Red herring   jargon for the preliminary prospectus because of the disclaimer printed in red on the cover, this is the preliminary prospectus which may be sent to potential purchasers of a new non-exempt securities issue during the 20-day cooling off period under the Securities Act of 1933. Legally, the preliminary prospectus does not offer the securities, since this is prohibited during the cooling off period. The red herring is used to get an indication of the public's interest in a security before the final price is set and the security issued. (see Cooling off period, Prospectus)

Redeemable bond   another name for a callable bond.

Redeemable security   a security that can only be bought from and sold back to the issuer. Mutual funds, unit investment trusts, Series EE, and Series HH saving bonds are redeemable securities. These are also described as non-negotiable. (compare Negotiable security)

Redemption   when the issuer of a debt security or preferred stock repays the principal or face value to the holder. Redemption occurs at a security's maturity date, or when a security is called, or when the holder exercises a security's put feature. (see Maturity date, Call feature, Put feature)

Redemption fee   a fee that some mutual funds may charge investors when they liquidate their shares. (see Back-end load, Contingent deferred sales charge)

Refunded debt   using the proceeds from a new issue bond to retire an outstanding bond that has a higher coupon rate.

Regional fund   a mutual fund or closed-end fund that invests in the negotiable securities of companies located in a specific geographic area.

Registered bond   the name of the person who owns the bond is recorded on the books of the issuer or the issuer's registrar. If a bond is fully registered, then both the principal amount and the interest payment amounts will appear in the issuer's records - hence this bond is termed "registered to principal and interest." Payments are sent directly by the paying agent to the registered holder. If a bond is registered as to principal only, then only the principal amount will appear on the issuer's records; such a bond has "bearer" coupons attached. (compare Bearer bond)

Registered Investment Adviser   abbreviated RIA, this is a person who is registered as an investment adviser with the SEC and/or the state. Individuals associated with RIAs must pass either the Series #65 or Series #66 examination (in most states).

Registered Options Principal   a manager who has passed a qualifying examination (either the FINRA/NYSE Series #9/10 Branch Manager Examination or the CBOE Series #4 Registered Options Principal Examination) that allows that individual to approve new options accounts and orders in options accounts (compare Senior Registered Options Principal, Compliance Registered Options Principal)

Registered Options Trader   also abbreviated "ROT," this is a floor trader on the CBOE who trades options solely for his own account. (see Floor trader; compare Floor broker)

Registered Representative also known as a broker or registered representative, an individual who is employed by a broker-dealer to handle customer accounts and to advise the public about investing in securities. This person must be registered with and licensed (Series #7) by FINRA. (see Account executive)

Registered securities 1) securities that are registered and held in customer's name at a brokerage firm; 2) securities that are registered in the customer's name on the books of the issuer or transfer agent; 3) securities that are registered with the SEC.

Registered to principal only bond a bond where the principal (face) amount is registered in the owner's name; but the bond has bearer coupons attached. Thus, anyone can clip the coupons and receive the interest payments; but the principal amount will be repaid only to the registered holder. No such bonds have been issued since 1983, after which all bonds issued in the United States must be fully registered. However, these bonds still trade in the market. (compare Fully registered bond, Bearer bond)

Registrar usually a commercial bank or trust company that is responsible for maintaining the integrity of the list of the names and addresses of a company's stockholders. The registrar is also responsible for insuring that the transfer agent does not over issue or under issue shares, as it transfers shares from seller to buyer. (see Transfer agent)

Registration statement the disclosure document that must be filed with the SEC under the Securities Act of 1933 by all companies planning to offer non-exempt securities to the public. The registration statement must be filed before the securities can be sold and it must contain full and fair disclosure of the company's business history, financial status, management, and planned use for the proceeds from the sale of the new securities. Most of the registration statement is a copy of the Prospectus to be given to investors. (see Exempt security, Non-exempt security, Prospectus)

Regressive tax   a tax, such as excise taxes and sales taxes, that remains at the same rate regardless of a person's income. Regressive taxes affect poor people more adversely because they take a larger percentage of their income. (compare Progressive tax)

Regular-way settlement   for corporate stocks, and bonds and municipal securities, the normal settlement method in which the securities must be delivered and paid for, no later than three business days after the trade date. There are, however, a few variations. For U.S. Government securities and most Agency securities, regular way settlement is the next business day. When trading options, regular way settlement is the next business day as well. (compare Cash settlement)

Regulation A   an exempt transaction under the Securities Act of 1933 that permits a non-exempt issuer to issue up to $5,000,000 worth of securities each year and remain exempt from having to register the securities with the SEC.

Regulation D   an exempt transaction under the Securities Act of 1933 that allows a private placement of securities to the public without the filing of a registration statement with the SEC. Under Regulation D, a private placement can be sold to an unlimited number of accredited (wealthy) investors, but only to a maximum of 35 non-accredited investors. (see Accredited investor)

Regulation G   the Federal Reserve rule that controls the extension of credit on non-exempt securities by anyone other than a broker or a bank. Please note that this regulation was rescinded in 1998; and its provisions were folded into Regulation U. (compare Regulation T, Regulation U)

Regulation SHO   an SEC rule effective in 2005 that imposes new short sale requirements. The short sale rule requiring an up-tick or up-bid is rescinded. The rule prohibits "naked short selling" and requires exchanges to maintain a "threshold list" of hard to borrow securities. If a threshold list security is sold short and the security is not delivered on settlement, the rule requires that the security be bought-in 10 business days after settlement (called 13 settlement days in the rule, since it counts from trade date).

Regulation T the Federal Reserve's regulation that controls the extension of credit on non-exempt securities from brokers to their customers. Regulation T defines the types of accounts in which transactions may occur; defines which securities are marginable; defines the initial margin requirements to establish securities positions in accounts; and sets maximum time periods for the collection of monies due from customers. (compare Regulation U)

Regulation U the Federal Reserve regulation that controls credit extended by banks to their customers, where securities are the collateral for the loan. Broker-dealers are the "customers" of banks under this definition, and Regulation U sets the amount or percentage of credit that a bank may extend to a broker-dealer who buys non-exempt securities on margin. (compare Regulation T)

Rehypothecation the repledging of customer margin securities to a bank by a broker-dealer to collateralize a broker loan. The hypothecation agreement signed by a customer to open a margin account permits the broker to repledge these securities to a bank for a loan. The maximum amount of customer securities that may be repledged is limited to an amount that does not exceed 140% of customer debit balances. (see Hypothecation, Broker loan rate)

Reinvestment risk the risk that the dividends, interest, and principal received from securities can only be invested at a lower rate of return than that earned from the previous investments. In other words, as the investment is being held, interest rates are going down, and reinvested monies are not earning as high a rate of return as the original investment.

REIT abbreviation for Real Estate Investment Trust. Regulated as a closed-end management company, REITs purchase different kinds of real estate investments such as buildings, mortgages, and short-term construction loans. REITs can invest in property (Equity REIT) or can buy mortgages and other real estate loans (Mortgage REIT). This security trades on the exchanges or in the OTC market.

Rejection   if a delivery of securities from one dealer is discovered not to be "good" on settlement date, then the accepting dealer can return the securities under his right of rejection for correction of the problem. (compare Reclamation)

Related portfolio   a portfolio that is controlled, directly or indirectly, by a member firm e.g., a mutual fund that is managed by a member firm.

REMIC   an acronym for Real Estate Mortgage Investment Conduit, this is essentially the same as a collateralized mortgage obligation (CMO, a REMIC provides an issuer with greater flexibility in grouping the underlying mortgages into many different classes, including maturity and risk, and thereby creating more tranches. (see CMO, tranch)

Reoffering price   in a competitive bid underwriting of a new issue municipal bond, the yield or price at which an underwriter sells the municipal bonds to the public after it has been awarded the bid (that is, bought the bonds from the municipality). The reoffering yield is typically set lower than the bond's coupon rate, thus the bond is priced at a premium over par the public. Since the underwriter's bid is usually for the par value of the bonds, the difference between par and the aggregate reoffering price (known as the "production") is the underwriter's spread, or gross profit. (see Production)

Reoffering scale   a listing of the prices or yields by maturity at which a new issue of municipal serial bonds is being sold to the public by an underwriter. The name "scale" derives from the fact that the yields "scale up" as the maturities lengthen on the issue (most municipal issues are serial bonds - that is, sequential maturities.) (see Reoffering yield)

Reoffering yield   in a competitive bid underwriting of a new issue municipal bond, the yield or price at which an underwriter sells the municipal bonds to the public after it has been awarded the bid (that is, bought the bonds from the municipality). The reoffering yield is typically set lower than the bond's coupon rate, thus the bond is priced at a premium over par the public. Since the underwriter's bid is usually for the par value of the bonds, the difference between par and the aggregate reoffering price (known as "production" is the underwriter's spread or gross profit. (see Production)

Reorganization (Reorg) department   part of a brokerage firm's operations or "back office" that is responsible for handling changes in a company's securities resulting from changes in its capitalization due to mergers, acquisitions, stock splits, conversions, exchange offers, tender offers, etc.

Repo   the commonly used name for a repurchase agreement.

Repurchase agreement (Repo)   where the Federal Reserve or another U.S. Government securities dealer buys securities from a dealer, promising to sell back the securities back for a higher price at a later date. "Repos" are a source of short-term financing for dealers needing cash. When the Fed initiates a repo with a member bank dealer, it is injecting cash into the banks, expanding credit availability. As a result, interest rates are likely to drop. The duration of a repo can range from overnight to weeks. (see Overnight repo, Reverse repurchase agreement)

Research report   any client communication that analyzes individual securities or companies if it provides information reasonably sufficient upon which to base an investment decision and is distributed to at least 15 persons.

Reserve maintenance fund   for municipal revenue bond issues, as stated in the "flow of funds" found in the trust indenture, a separate account established to receive any excess payments made by the issuer after required deposits have been made to the maintenance fund. (see Flow of funds)

Reserve requirement   the percentage of demand deposits and time deposits that the Federal Reserve requires every member bank to keep on deposit in its own vault or in the vaults of one of the Fed's regional banks. Each member bank must compute its reserve every Wednesday and report it to the Fed. If a bank finds itself below the requirement, it must borrow money overnight in the Federal Funds market to temporarily meet the requirement. (see Federal funds)

Reset bond   a debt security whose interest rate is reset periodically (e.g., semi-annually, annually) to reflect current interest rates, as determined by a formula specified in the bond's trust indenture. Unlike fixed rate debt, whose price moves inversely with market interest rate movements; the interest rate on reset bonds changes with market interest rates, hence the price stays at par.

Resistance level   a price level to which a stock or the market rises (and then falls from) repeatedly. Selling increases as a stock's price approaches this level, so the stock has resistance to further upward price moves, hence the name. If a stock's price breaks the resistance level, then it is believed by technical analysts that there are still buyers, without the same level of sellers, so there will be a strong upward price movement in the stock due to the excess of buyers in the market. (compare Support level)

Restricted account   a margin account whose equity is less than the Federal Reserve Board's Regulation T initial margin requirement of 50% (but greater than the NASD/NYSE (now merged into FINRA) minimum maintenance margin of 25% for a long account and 30% for a short account). When an account is "restricted," there are limits on the withdrawal of funds when securities are sold from the account. Specifically, 50% of the proceeds of any sale must be retained in the account when securities are sold from a restricted account. This is known as the retention requirement. (see Retention requirement)

Restricted stock   stock, usually issued directly to the officers or directors of a corporation in a private placement, that has not been registered with the SEC. These shares are privately placed under Regulation D, and thus are exempt from registration. Resales of restricted securities in the public markets must comply with the provisions of SEC Rule 144 (see Rule 144).

Restriction   under Regulation T, the amount by which a margin account is below 50% initial margin. When an account is restricted, there are limits on the cash withdrawals that may be made from the account when securities positions are liquidated.

Retained earnings the portion of a company's earnings that the Board of Directors does not pay out as dividends to the common stockholders. Retained earnings are reinvested in the company's operations. (see Earnings per share, Dividend)

Retention requirement in a restricted margin account (one that is below 50% Regulation T initial margin), the portion of any sale amount that must be retained in the account and which cannot be withdrawn. The retention requirement is currently 50%. (see Restricted account)

Return on common equity the ratio of a corporation's earnings for common shareholders to total common stockholders' equity. (see Earnings for common, Common stockholders' equity)

Revdex a yield to maturity index published by the Bond Buyer, it is the average yield of 25 selected revenue bonds with 30 years to maturity, all rated A or better. (compare Bond Buyer index)

Revenue anticipation note (RAN) a short-term municipal security issued in anticipation of receiving revenues from sources other than income or property taxes. When received, this revenue will be used to repay the note. (compare Bond anticipation note, Construction loan note, Tax anticipation note, Tax and revenue anticipation note)

Revenue bond a municipal bond whose proceeds will be used to build a revenue-producing facility, such as a toll road or bridge, a sports arena, or a hospital. The interest payments and principal repayments will be made from the revenues generated by this enterprise activity. Revenue bonds are described as being self-supporting, since they "pay their own way" and are not paid from tax collections. Interest from some non-essential use, private purpose revenue bonds may be subject to the alternative minimum tax (AMT) or regular income tax. (compare General Obligation bond)

Revenue fund   the collection account provided for under the "flow of funds" in a revenue bond trust indenture to collect all monies generated by a revenue producing facility. Once the monies are accounted for, disbursements are made under the flow of funds as set forth in the revenue bond trust indenture. (see Flow of funds)

Revenue pledge   a protective covenant found in a revenue bond trust indenture, under a revenue pledge, the issuer pledges the revenues from the facility to the bondholders, either under a Gross revenue pledge (the bondholders have first claim on revenues prior to paying operation and maintenance); or a net revenue pledge (the bondholders have a claim on revenues only after operation and maintenance is paid). (see Gross revenue pledge, Net revenue pledge)

Reverse repo   the commonly used slang for a reverse repurchase agreement, this is where the Federal Reserve sells U.S. Government and other eligible securities to bank dealers, with an agreement to buy back the securities, usually the next day. For 1 day, the bank dealers are drained of cash, which reduces the banks' funds that they can lend. This action tightens credit, and raises interest rates - notably the Fed funds rate. (see Fed funds rate; compare Repurchase agreement)

Reverse repurchase agreement   this is where the Federal Reserve sells U.S. Government and other eligible securities to bank dealers, with an agreement to buy back the securities, usually the next day. For 1 day, the bank dealers are drained of cash, which reduces the banks' funds that they can lend. This action tightens credit, and raises interest rates - notably the Fed funds rate. (see Federal funds rate; compare Repurchase agreement).

Reverse stock split   a stock split that is used to increase, rather than decrease, the market price of an issuer's stock. For example, if an issuer has 5,000,000 common shares outstanding at $1 each; and there is a 1:5 reverse split, on the ex date there will be 1,000,000 shares outstanding at $5 each.

Reversionary working interest   in an oil and gas program, a sharing arrangement where the general partner bears none of the costs, but defers taking a percentage of oil revenue until all costs paid by the limited partners are recovered. This is also known as a Subordinated Royalty Interest. (compare Disproportionate sharing arrangement, Overriding royalty interest, Net profits interest)

RIA   abbreviation for a Registered Investment Adviser, this is a person who is registered as an investment adviser with the SEC and/or the state. Individuals associated with RIAs must pass either the Series #65 or Series #66 examination (in most states).

Right   also called a subscription right, a right allows common stockholders to maintain their same percentage of ownership in a company that is issuing new stock. The right entitles existing shareholders to subscribe to the new shares of the company before they are offered to the public. The price (known as the subscription price) at which the new shares will be sold to the existing stockholders is lower than the stock's current market price - with the discount to the shareholders reflecting the spread that an underwriter would take to sell the shares to other investors. Rights can be exercised; or can be sold for value in the market. They typically expire within 90 days of issuance. (see Preemptive right)

Right of accumulation   a reduction in the sales charge on a mutual fund purchase when the value of an investor's shares, when accumulated with a current purchase, reaches a breakpoint. (see Breakpoint)

Rights agent   usually the transfer agent, the rights agent accepts the monies (along with the appropriate number of rights certificates) for subscriptions to new shares via a rights offering and issues the new shares to the subscribers.

Rights offering   the method and terms by which preemptive rights to subscribe to newly issued common shares are distributed to a company's existing common shareholders. (see Preemptive right)

Risk arbitrage   the simultaneous purchase and sale of the shares of two companies in anticipation of, or upon the announcement, of a merger or acquisition where payment will be made in stock. In such a case, the stock of the company to be acquired rises in price, while the stock of the acquirer typically stays the same, or falls slightly. To profit, a risk arbitrageur would buy the shares of the cheaper target company; and sell short the shares of the more expensive acquiring company. If the takeover goes through, each share of the target company is exchanged for share(s) of the acquiring company; which can be used to replace the short (borrowed) position.

The "risk" in such a transaction is that the deal may fall through, leaving the arbitrageur with a loss on each separate position. (see Merger, Acquisition

Risk adjusted rate of return   the excess return that can be achieved by investing in a chosen asset class, over and above that can be achieved by investing in an asset class that has no risk, such as Treasury Bills. (see Risk free rate of return; compare Risk premium)

Risk free rate of return   the return that can be achieved by investing in an asset class that has no risk, such as Treasury Bills.

Risk premium   the excess return that can be achieved by investing in specific securities, as compared to a benchmark portfolio. (compare Risk-adjusted rate of return)

Riskless transaction   a transaction that a broker-dealer performs for a customer that involves no risk to the dealer. An OTC dealer that buys a stock into its inventory in order to fill a customer's existing buy order engages in a riskless transaction. This is also known as a simultaneous transaction.

Roth IRA   a type of Individual Retirement Account that allows an individual to contribute up to $5,000 (for the year 2008); but no tax deduction is available. If the investment is held for at least 5 years; and if the person is at least age 59 1/2, distributions are not taxable. (compare IRA, Education IRA)

Round-lot trade a trade of a minimum normal trading unit size. For common and preferred stock, a trade involving 100 shares. For municipal bonds, a trade of $100,000 face value bonds. For corporate bonds, a trade of $5,000 face value bonds. (compare Odd lot)

Rule 10-b-5 under the Securities and Exchange Act of 1934, the "catch-all" fraud rule, that states that any action taken in the secondary market that is manipulative, though not specifically defined under the Act, still is considered to be fraudulent.

Rule 144 an SEC rule that permits the holders of private placement "restricted" shares to resell these securities in the public markets without filing a registration statement, if the issuer has "gone public." Rule 144 requires public notice of the sale; places limitations on the timing of the sales; and limits the amount that can be sold. Holders of "control" stock (shares purchased by officers of the issuer in the open market) also come under most of the Rule 144 limitations. (see Restricted stock, Control stock)

Rule 144A not to be confused with Rule 144, this rule permits large private placement offerings to be made to Qualified Institutional Buyers (QIBs) who may trade these securities among themselves without having to register the securities. (see QIB)

Rule 145 an SEC rule that requires issuers to file registration statements and issue prospectuses to investors for securities that arise out of mergers and divestitures. The rule does not apply to securities issued as the result of stock dividends or stock splits, however.

Rule 147 the SEC rule that spells out the requirements for an issuer to obtain an exemption from registration for a new issue because the offering will be made only in 1 state (an intrastate exemption). 100% of the issue must be sold solely to state residents to obtain the exemption.

Rule 11A-c-1-6   requires member firms to disclose to customers, upon request, the market venues to which the member firm sent that customer's orders for the prior 6 months; whether the orders were directed to a specific marketplace by the customer or non-directed (meaning the member firm got to choose where the order was executed); and the time of each transaction that resulted from these orders.

Rules 15-g-1 through 15-g-6   commonly known as the "penny stock rule," a set of SEC rules that have been adopted by FINRA/NASD requiring that any customers who are solicited to buy a non-exchange, non-NASDAQ stock under $5, sign a detailed suitability statement that prominently discloses the high risks involved with such a security, prior to confirmation of sale.

Rule 415   known as the "shelf registration rule," this is a streamlined registration process under the Securities Act of 1933 for large, established companies. Rather than having to file a registration statement and complete a 20 day cooling off period for each new securities offering, the issuer files a blanket registration statement with the SEC that goes on the SEC's "shelf" for 2 years. Once the "shelf" filing is made, by giving 2 days' notice to the SEC, the issuer can sell new securities in the market. This procedure is much faster and cheaper.

S

s   a letter on the Consolidated Tape that denotes the sale of a round lot of stock. When the sale involves more than one round lot, a number precedes the letter - e.g., 4s denotes the sale of four round lots (400 shares). (see Consolidated tape)

s/s   usually stacked vertically without the slash, this ticker symbol indicates the sale of a 10 share lot of cabinet stock. Cabinet stocks are either very expensive shares; or companies that are infrequently traded on the NYSE. (see Cabinet stock)

Safe harbor   a provision included in a regulatory code that, if its conditions are met, allows that the benefit given by that provision cannot be challenged. Thus, anyone who follows the requirements of the provision is given a "safe harbor" from prosecution.

Sales charge   the percentage of the public offering price that many mutual funds charge when an investor buys shares. While this percentage is usually deducted up front, it can be deducted when a person withdraws from the fund. In the latter case, this is a contingent deferred sales charge. By FINRA/NASD rule, the maximum sales charge on a mutual fund is 8.5% of the public offering price. In reality, actual sales charges are much lower, due to competition in the marketplace. Mutual funds with sales charges are known as load funds. Those without sales charges are called no-load funds.

Sales proceeds   for purposes of computing a capital gain or loss, the price at which a security is sold, net of any commissions or mark-downs charged. If a writer of a call is exercised, selling the stock, the resultant sale proceeds is the strike price plus premium received; if the buyer of a put exercises, selling the stock, the resultant sale proceeds is the strike price minus premium received.

Sallie Mae   the commonly used name for a security issued by the Student Loan Marketing Association (SLMA). Sallie Mae is a privatized government agency whose stock is listed on the NYSE that buys student loans from originating financial institutions. Sallie Mae sells notes and bonds to finance this activity.

SAR   the Suspicious Activities Report, which must be filed by financial institutions with FinCEN (Financial Crimes Enforcement Network) when it is suspected that a customer is money laundering.

Sarbanes-Oxley Act of 2002   passed in response to the wave of scandals that became evident after the great market meltdown of 2000, this Act tightened corporate reporting rules including faster reporting of insider trades, mandated that research analysts be separated from broker-dealer investment banking functions, and increased auditor liability for fraudulent corporate actions.

Saucer formation   a stock price charting that shows a stock's price gently bottoming out and then gently rising over time, creating a saucer shape. An inverted saucer is a stock price charting that shows a stock's price gently topping out and then gently falling over time, creating an upside-down saucer shape.

Savings and Loan issue   a security issued by a Savings and Loan Association. S&Ls are formed to act as local lenders, accepting deposits and giving mortgage loans to local homeowners.

Savings bonds   Series EE and Series HH bonds issued by the U.S. Government. These are redeemable securities; they are non-negotiable and do not trade. Interest on the bonds is exempt from state and local taxes, and no federal taxes are due on the Series EE bonds until redemption.

Scale   also called the reoffering scale, the listing of the prices or yields at which a new issue municipal bond is sold to the public. The listing gets its name because it is organized by maturity (since most municipal issues are serial bonds), and the yields increase as the maturities lengthen - so it "scales up" with maturity. The scale appears in the Official Statement (disclosure document) of the municipal issue. (see Reoffering yield)

SEC   abbreviation for the Securities and Exchange Commission. Established in 1934 as the regulatory authority of the securities industry, the SEC is responsible for interpreting, supervising, and enforcing compliance with the provisions of the various securities acts.

Second market   the trading market (secondary market) is sub-categorized into the First, Second, Third, and Fourth markets. This is the order of the development of these markets in the United States. The Second Market is the OTC (over-the-counter) market, where securities that are not listed on an exchange floor trade. FINRA/NASD regulates the Second Market. Securities traded OTC include government and agency bonds; municipal bonds; and NASDAQ and non-NASDAQ securities. The Second Market should not be confused with the secondary market - which encompasses the entire trading market for issued securities.

Second mortgage bond   a secured corporate bond that is backed by a second mortgage on real property. These bonds have second claim (a "junior lien") to the collateral backing the bonds; the First mortgage (a "senior lien") bonds issued by the corporation have a prior claim. Mortgage bonds are typically issued by utilities. (compare First mortgage bond)

Second party   regarding brokerage accounts, the parties to the account are: First Party - Brokerage Firm; Second Party - Customer; Third Party - Anyone other than the Brokerage Firm or Customer.

Secondary market   also called the aftermarket, a collective term for the markets - exchange and OTC - in which securities trade after they are issued to the public. Proceeds from transactions in this market go to the selling investor. The secondary market is made up of four markets: the First, Second, Third and Fourth markets. (see First market, Second market, Third market, Fourth market; compare Primary market)

Secondary market joint account   in the municipal trading market, a syndicate formed to buy a large block of bonds in the secondary market, usually from a large institution that wishes to "unload" a block of bonds at an attractive price. By joining together, the syndicate can raise enough money to buy this large block of bonds. The syndicate then reoffers the bonds to other dealers by publishing a single quote for the bonds in the Blue List. (see Blue list)

Secondary offering   the sale (or more accurately resale) to the general public in a prospectus offering under the provisions of the Securities Act of 1933 of securities previously issued to large investors, such as institutions and insiders. The net proceeds of the offering go to the selling shareholders. (compare Initial public offering, Primary offering)

Section 529 plan a state-sponsored education savings plan that allows non-tax deductible contributions to be made to a trust to pay for a beneficiary's qualified higher education expenses. Maximum annual contributions and funding are set by each state. Earnings build tax deferred and distributions to pay for qualified higher education expenses are not taxable.

Section 8 housing   named after the "Section 8" program, where the federal government subsidized all of the annual costs of the operation of low income housing. Bonds used to build "Section 8" housing are referred to as New housing authority bonds, Public housing authority bonds, or "Section 8" bonds. These bonds are no longer issued. (see Public housing authority bond)

Sector fund   a management company that invests in one industry or segment of an industry. Because this type of fund is often not diversified, it has higher levels of non-systematic risk. (see Diversified fund, non-systematic risk)

Secured bond   a bond that is backed by real property, tangible assets, or other securities. Types of secured bonds include mortgage bonds, equipment trust certificates and collateral trust certificates. The specific collateral backing the bond must be stated in the Trust Indenture of the bond. (see Mortgage bond, Equipment trust certificate, Collateral trust certificate; compare Unsecured bond))

Securities Act of 1933   the federal regulation aimed at curbing manipulation and fraud in the new issue market. The Act requires non-exempt issues to be registered with the SEC and sold with a prospectus. (see Non-exempt security, Prospectus)

Securities and Exchange Act of 1934   the federal regulation to curb manipulation and fraud in the trading (secondary) markets. The Act consists of a broad array of provisions to: curb insider abuses; require registration and self-regulation of exchanges under SEC oversight; require registration of, member firms, and their sales employees; require issuers to make public their financial statements; give the Federal Reserve the power to set margins; and numerous rules to curb manipulative market practices.

Securities and Exchange Commission   established in 1934, under the Securities and Exchange Act of 1934, this is the regulatory authority over the securities industry. The SEC is responsible for interpreting, supervising, and enforcing compliance with the provisions of the various securities acts.

Securities Investor Protection Act of 1970   created SIPC - Securities Investor Protection Corporation, which insures customer accounts against loss if a broker-dealer fails. Coverage limits are $500,000 of equity in an account, inclusive of maximum cash coverage of $100,000.

Securities Investor Protection Corporation   a non-profit government sponsored corporation, SIPC insures customer accounts against loss if a broker-dealer fails. Coverage limits are $500,000 of equity in an account, inclusive of maximum cash coverage of $100,000.

Self Regulatory Organization   also known as an "SRO," this is an exchange that is registered with the SEC under the Securities and Exchange Act of 1934, and which regulates itself under SEC oversight. For example, the CBOE and FINRA are SROs.

Self-supporting debt   a municipal revenue bond that pays debt service (both interest and principal) from the revenues generated from an enterprise activity. Thus, it "pays its own way," so it is self-supporting. The bond has no claim on tax collections, which would make the bond "non-self supporting" - that is, carried on the backs of the taxpayers. (compare General obligation bond, Non-self supporting debt)

Sell long   selling securities that a customer owns - i.e., liquidating an existing long position. (compare Sell short)

Sell short   selling securities in anticipation of a market decline. The customer borrows the securities to be sold through his or her brokerage firm with the intent of buying them back (and replacing them to the lender) once the price has declined. (compare Sell long)

Seller's option settlement   settlement of a securities transaction that takes place on a date later than regular way settlement, with the actual settlement date set by the seller. (compare Regular way settlement)

Selling concession   1) in a negotiated underwriting, that portion of the underwriting spread which the managing underwriter, with the agreement of the syndicate members, concedes or gives to the selling group members for each new issue security they sell directly to the public. (see Underwriter's concession, Selling group); 2) in a competitive bid municipal bond underwriting, that portion of the total takedown on a new issue municipal bond that a selling group member receives for each bond it sells to the public. (see Total takedown, Additional takedown)

Selling group   brokerage firms who participate in a new issue underwriting totally in an agency capacity - i.e., they are responsible for selling the new issue only and share none of the financial liability. The selling group receives a selling concession on each security sold. (see Selling concession)

Selling long   selling off or liquidating stock positions that an investor owns.

Selling power   in a short margin account, the amount of additional securities that can be sold short without making a deposit of funds. Selling power is 2 times the SMA in the account (compare Buying power)

Selling short   a strategy used by investors to profit from a price decline; where an investor sells securities that he or she has borrowed, with the intention of repurchasing them later at a lower price, replacing the borrowed shares for a profit. To sell short, a margin deposit is required as assurance that the customer will later buy back and replace the borrowed shares.

Senior lien bond a secured corporate bond that is backed by a first, or senior, lien on real property. This is also called a First Mortgage bond; because there can be Second mortgage bonds issued ("junior lien bonds") that have a lower claim priority on the property. Mortgage bonds are typically issued by utilities. (compare Junior lien bond)

Senior Registered Options Principal a CBOE designation for a person who has passed the Series #4 examination. This is an individual who is located in the firm's supervisory office, who is responsible for overseeing options accounts, reviewing selected new accounts; and reviewing options transactions in accounts. This person oversees the Registered Options Principals (FINRA/NASD firms); or Branch Office Managers (FINRA/NYSE firms); in the branch locations.

Senior security preferred stock and bonds that are senior to common stock as to their claim on earnings of the company, and on corporate assets in a liquidation. (compare Junior security)

Sentiment indicators statistics used to measure the bullish or bearish mood of the market and its investors. Measures of investor sentiment include the Consumer confidence index; short interest levels; and put/call ratio. (see Consumer confidence index, Short interest, Put/Call ratio)

SEP-IRA a Simplified Employee Pension plan, designed especially for small businesses, this is a pension plan in which the employer opens an IRA for each employee and makes a contribution on his or her behalf. While the contribution limits are higher than those for a regular IRA, if the employer contributes less than the maximum allowed under a regular IRA, then the employee can make up the difference. A SEP requires less administration and filing requirements than a regular corporate qualified pension plan.

Separate account the account in which a variable annuity investor's monies are used to buy designated mutual fund shares. The performance of the mutual fund held in the separate account will determine the amount of the annuity to be received. It is called a separate account because its assets are kept separate from the insurance company's other investments, which are held in the general account of the insurance company.

Serial bond   a bond, usually a municipal bond, that is issued all at one time and then matures in installments over a number of years - hence, it has serial maturities. (compare Series bond, Term bond)

Series #6 license   the investment companies/ variable annuities license, this allows a person to sell mutual funds; unit investment trusts; and initial public offerings of closed-end funds to investors. To sell other securities, or to trade closed-end funds, requires the broader Series #7 license.

Series #7 license   the general securities license that allows an individual to sell any security.

Series #63 license   the state license for an individual to sell securities (be an "agent") in a state.

Series #65 license   the state license for an individual to be an investment adviser representative in a state.

Series #66 license   the state license for an individual to be both an agent and investment adviser representative in a state.

Series bond   a bond that is issued in installments over a number of years, but all of the bonds in the issue mature at the same time. Usually issued to fund construction projects in which the money is needed in phases over a long period of time, bonds with this type of structure are rarely issued today. (compare Serial bond, Term bond)

Series EE bonds   non-negotiable U.S. Government savings bonds that are purchased at 50 percent of face value and which mature at face value. The purchaser receives no interest until the bonds are redeemed. Taxes are paid at redemption. Series EE bonds come in denominations of $50 to $10,000. These are redeemable securities that do not trade.

Series HH bonds   non-negotiable U.S. Government savings bonds that are purchased at face value by any holder of a Series EE bond that wishes to exchange one bond for the other. Whereas Series EE bonds are bought at a discount, and mature at par, with the difference being the interest earned; Series HH bonds are issued at par and pay interest semi-annually to the bondholder. (see Series EE bonds)

Service well   in an oil and gas income program, a second well drilled near an existing well that is used to inject water and chemicals into the ground to bring up more oil. (see Income oil and gas program)

Settlement date   the date on which the orderly exchange of monies and securities occurs following a purchase or sale. (see Cash settlement, Regular way settlement)

Shelf registration   an amendment to the Securities Act of 1933 called Rule 415, permitting large, established, public corporations to maintain and regularly update a registration statement "on the shelves" of the SEC that can be used to issue securities when market conditions are favorable. For a publicly held company, maintaining a shelf registration is less costly and restrictive than following the normal registration procedures for a new issue. (see Rule 415)

Short against the box   an end-of-the-year tax strategy that enables an investor to lock in a gain on a profitable long position but, under tax law revisions of 1997, generally does not defer taxation of the gain. The investor borrows and sells short a number of shares equal to his or her profitable long position at the current market price. This locks in the gain, but taxes are due at this point. This transaction is effected in an Arbitrage Account, which has a very low margin requirement because this is, essentially, a riskless transaction. (see Arbitrage account)

Short bond   a bond with less than two years left to maturity. (compare Medium term bond, Long bond)

Short call   an option contract that obligates the investor to deliver common stock (or other underlying instrument) at a fixed price, good until a fixed expiration date. For taking on this obligation, the seller of the call receives a premium. (compare Long call)

Short call spread   the sale of a lower strike price call option; and the purchase of a higher strike price call option; on the same underlying security. This is a bear market strategy. In a falling market, both calls expire "out the money." There is a profit from the net premium credit received. Spreads are gain limiting and loss limiting positions. (compare Long call spread)

Short coupon bond   a new issue bond whose first coupon payment will encompass less than six months of interest. Since most bonds pay interest on January 1st and July 1st (very easy to remember these dates!), if such a bond is issued, say in November, the first interest payment will occur on January 1st, covering 2 months of interest (November and December. Thereafter, the bond pays interest on the regular semi-annual January 1st and July 1st dates. This is also called an "odd first interest payment."

Short cover   the closing of a short stock position by purchasing the shares in the market and using these to replace the shares that were borrowed to effect the short sale. (see Short sale)

Short interest   the total level of uncovered short sales, reported each month by the exchanges. A very large short interest indicates that the market is "oversold" and is likely to turn upwards. A very low short interest indicates that the market is "overbought" and is likely to turn downwards. This is a contrary technical indicator. (see Short sale, Overbought market, Oversold market)

Short interest ratio   a calculation (a stock's short interest divided by its average daily trading volume) used to determine the number of days it would take to cover, or buy-in, the number of shares that investors have sold short. (see Short interest)

Short margin account   a margin account in which a customer sells short securities. All short sales must be performed in a margin account. (see Sell short; compare Long margin account)

Short market value   the market value of securities that are sold short in a margin account. The value of these securities is marked to market daily. (see Mark to market, Short margin account)

Short position   phrase denoting a security position created by selling borrowed securities in anticipation of a market price decline. The short seller promises to buy back the position upon demand of the brokerage firm. To take a short position requires a margin deposit. (compare Long position)

Short put   an option contract that obligates the investor to buy common stock (or another underlying instrument) at a fixed price, good until a fixed expiration date. For taking on this obligation, the seller of the put receives a premium. (compare Long put)

Short put spread   the sale of a higher strike price put option; and the purchase of a lower strike price put option; on the same underlying security. This is a bull market strategy, also termed a Bull Put Spread. In a rising market, both puts expire "out the money." There is a profit from the net premium credit received. Spreads are gain limiting and loss limiting positions. (compare Long put spread)

Short sale   the sale of borrowed securities, with the intention of buying back the securities later at a lower price and replacing the borrowed shares. As a good faith deposit that the borrowed shares will be replaced, the customer must make a margin deposit. (see Sell short; compare Long sale)

Short spread   an option spread in which the investor simultaneously buys the option with the lower premium and sells the same type of option with the higher premium. The net difference between the lower premium paid and the higher premium received is the credit. This type of spread is profitable if the difference between the premiums narrows or if both options expire. (see Spread; compare Long spread)

Short straddle   the sale of a call and a put option on the same underlying security, with the same strike price and expiration. This option strategy is used when it is expected that the market will be stable. (compare Long straddle)

Short swing profit   1) under IRS rules, a gain on an asset sold within 1 year of acquisition; 2) under SEC rules, a profit achieved within 6 months by an insider trading his or her own company's stock, that must be "disgorged" and repaid to the company.

Short tender rule   an SEC rule that states that if a company tenders for its shares, only those persons with net long positions can tender. Anyone who is net zero the stock (e.g., short against the box) or net short cannot tender. (see Short against the box, Tender offer)

Short term bond   any debt obligation with one year or less left to maturity - this is a money market instrument. (compare Medium term bond, Long bond)

Short term capital gain (loss)   a gain or loss on an asset held for 1 year or less. Short term capital gains are taxed at higher rates than long term capital gains. (see Long term capital gain (loss))

Sides of the market   the market has 2 "sides" - the "up" or "bull" side; and the "down" or "bear" side. Bull market strategies include long stock positions, long calls and short puts. Bear market strategies include short stock positions, long puts and short calls.

Simplified Employee Pension plan   designed especially for small businesses, this is a pension plan in which the employer opens an IRA for each employee and makes a contribution on his or her behalf. While the contribution limits are higher than those for a regular IRA, if the employer contributes less than the maximum allowed under a regular IRA, then the employee can make up the difference. A SEP requires less administration and filing requirements than a regular corporate qualified pension plan.

Simultaneous transaction also known as a riskless principal transaction, a broker-dealer, upon receiving a customer order to buy, buys the security into the firm's inventory; and then immediately sells that security out of inventory to the customer with a mark-up. The broker-dealer is engaging in a simultaneous transaction. (compare Proceeds transaction, Arbitrage)

Single Book NASDAQ's new in 2007 automated trading system that merged the previous SuperMontage trading platform with the BRUT and INET (Instinet) ECN trading platforms purchased by NASDAQ.

Sinking fund for municipal bond issues, a separate account where periodic deposits are made by the issuer to meet required debt service payments of both interest and principal. (see Flow of funds)

Sinking fund call under the terms of the call covenant found in the bond contract or trust indenture, the issuer is obligated to call in a portion of a bond issue at regular pre-determined intervals, using the accumulated monies that have been deposited to the sinking fund. The actual bonds called are determined randomly. (see Sinking fund provision; compare In-whole call, Catastrophe call)

Sinking fund provision a feature that requires an issuer to regularly deposit funds into an escrow account that will eventually be used to redeem or repurchase the outstanding preferred issue or bond issue. The schedule and amount of payments into the sinking fund depends on the terms of the security. (see Debt service)

SIPC acronym for Securities Investor Protection Corporation, a government-sponsored private corporation created in 1970 that provides insurance protection for the customers of broker-dealers that go bankrupt. Each customer's account is covered for up to $500,000, of which no more than $100,000 can be cash. (compare FDIC)

SLD   an abbreviation appearing next to a stock's symbol on the ticker tape indicating that the stock was "Sold" (only sellers report to the tape), but that the trade was reported late to the tape, so this is not a current trading price for that security

SMA   abbreviation for Special Memorandum Account, this is the customer's available unused credit line in a margin account.

Small Business Investment Company   an exempt issue under the Securities Act of 1933, an investment company formed under SBA (Small Business Administration) rules to invest in minority businesses

SPDR   acronym for the Standard and Poor's 500 Index Exchange Traded Fund. Commonly referred to as the "Spider," it trades under the symbol SPY.

Special assessment bond   a municipal bond that is paid off by tax assessments on the beneficiaries of a municipal improvement.

Special memorandum account (SMA)   an account used to show the excess equity that an investor has in a margin account. This account is, in reality, a credit line against the increased equity of securities bought or sold short in a margin account.

Special situation fund   a management company that invests in companies that are candidates for takeover or those that are emerging from bankruptcy.

Special tax bond   a municipal bond that is paid from taxes other than ad valorem taxes. Typically, excise taxes, e.g., taxes on alcohol, tobacco, and gasoline, are the sources of revenue used to service the debt.

Specialist an exchange member located at the trading post, responsible for maintaining a fair and orderly market in the stock(s) assigned to him or her by the exchange. This person "specializes" in making a market in the stock, hence the name. Specialists buy and sell that stock for their own account, making a continuous market in the stock. In addition, the Specialist performs a second function by maintaining the "book" of open orders for other retail brokerage firms. On the Specialist's book are placed the orders that are "away from the current market" (limit, stop, and stop limit orders). These are executed by the Specialist for the retail broker when the market reaches the price specified on the order. In this capacity, the Specialist is acting as a "broker's broker." (compare Floor broker, Competitive trader)

Specialist's book the electronic display book on which the Specialist holds orders that have been placed away from a stock's current market - e.g., limit orders, stop orders, stop-limit orders. When the price of the stock moves to the price specified in the order, the Specialist executes the order for the retail member firm that placed the order. In this function, the Specialist acts as a "broker's broker," since he or she is a broker handling orders for retail brokerage firms. (see Specialist)

Specialty fund an investment company that invests in one industry or geographic area.

Specific identification a method of determining capital gain or loss on the sale of securities, where the investor can specify the securities that were sold. If the investor specifies the securities with the highest cost basis to be sold, then the resultant capital gain will be smaller; or the capital loss will be larger. If specific identification is not used, then FIFO - first in, first out, must be used. Also, specific identification cannot be used if a "wash sale" results (FIFO must be used). (see Wash sale rule)

SPIDER commonly used name for the Standard and Poor's 500 Index Exchange Traded Fund, an index fund that is exchange traded under the symbol SPY.

Spin off   a corporation that has a subsidiary that it feels will perform better as an independent company, may "spin-off" that business by giving its existing shareholders the subsidiary as a new independent company in a separate stock offering. For example, in 2006, American Express "spun-off" its brokerage operation (Ameriprise Financial Services) to its shareholders as a separate operating company.

Sponsor   for mutual funds, the sponsor is the fund company, also known as the fund underwriter. For limited partnerships, the sponsor is the organizer of the partnership, and is usually the general partner in the venture.

Sponsored ADR   an American Depositary Receipt in which the foreign company is directly involved, that is, sponsors the depositing of its shares with the bank that acts as trustee, registering the securities with the SEC, and issuing its receipts in the United States. Such companies comply with SEC reporting requirements in the United States. The larger exchanges, such as the NYSE, will only list "sponsored" ADRs. By increasing common practice, sponsored ADRs are called American Depositary Shares (ADSs). (see American Depositary Receipt; compare Unsponsored ADR)

Spot settlement   a means of settling foreign currency trades, spot trades settle in either 1 or 2 business days after trade date (trades of the more actively traded currencies settle in 1 business day; trades of the less actively traded currencies settle in 2 business days). (compare Forward settlement)

Spread   1) the gross compensation that an underwriter receives for distributing a new issue; 2) on a competitive bid new issue municipal bond, the difference between the total dollar amount the underwriting syndicate will receive when it sells the bonds to the public (this total is known as the production); and the total amount that the underwriter bids to purchase the bonds from the issuer. In mathematical terms, the spread on a new issue municipal bond is the production minus the bid (see Production, Competitive municipal bid); 3) the difference between the bid and ask prices for a security; 4) in options, a strategy involving buying and selling calls simultaneously on the same stock; or buying and selling puts simultaneously on the same stock. If only the expiration dates of the calls (or puts) are different, then the strategy is called a horizontal spread (or time or calendar spread). If only the strike prices of the calls (or puts) are different, then the strategy is called a vertical spread or price spread. If both the expiration dates and the strike prices are different on the calls (or puts), the strategy is known as a diagonal spread.

Spread order   an order to buy and sell the same type of option contract at different strike prices and / or expirations. Because the filling of the order requires that 2 trades be completed at the same time, these orders are given priority on the CBOE floor. (see Spread priority rule)

Spread priority rule   a rule of the Chicago Board Options Exchange that gives any "one-to-one" order priority on the exchange floor over equivalent single orders. "One-to-one" orders require that 2 "legs" of a position be filled to complete the order - these are spread and straddle orders. This rule makes it easier for traders to get both "legs" of the order filled to complete the spread or straddle position. (see Spread, Straddle)

SPX   the symbol for stock index options on the Standard & Poor's 500 index, traded on the CBOE.

Stabilization   during the sale of a new issue, the lead underwriter is permitted to put a "floor" on the price of the security in the aftermarket by placing a "stabilizing" bid in the trading market for the issue. This is the only legal form of market manipulation. Stabilizing bids are permitted at, or below, the Public Offering Price of the new issue - never above.

Stabilizing bid   the price, at or just below a new issue's public offering price, at which the lead underwriter will repurchase the issue in the secondary market while he or she is stabilizing the price of the new issue. (see Stabilization)

Stand-by commitment   used in a rights offering, an underwriting commitment in which an investment banker makes a firm commitment to stand by, ready to buy any of the unsold shares after the issuer attempts to sell its new shares to existing shareholders who have been granted subscription rights. In this manner, the corporation is assured of raising the full amount of money needed. (see Rights offering, Firm commitment)

Standard and Poor's 100 Index option   an index option contract that consists of 100 of the 500 stocks in the Standard and Poor's 500 index, this was the first index option contract traded. The Standard and Poor's 100 Index Option and the somewhat newer S&P 500 Index Option are the most popular options contracts in the world. The contract trades on the CBOE under the symbol OEX (Options Exchange Index).

Standard and Poor's 500 Index   a weighted index that overwhelmingly includes the largest issues that trade on the New York Stock Exchange, and some NASDAQ issues. It consists of about 400 industrial stocks, with the balance of the index composed of transportation, utility, and financial issues.

Standard and Poor's Corporation   one of the independent companies that rate the risk of default and the quality of the cash flow or assets backing fixed income issues - bonds, preferred stocks, and commercial paper. The three ratings services include (from largest to smallest) Moody's Investors Service, Standard and Poor's, and Fitch's.

Stated value   another term for par value. (see Par value)

Stated yield   the stated rate of interest, as a percentage of par value, that is paid on a fixed income security. This is the same as the coupon rate or nominal yield. (see Coupon rate, Nominal yield)

Statement   a summary of all transactions in an investor's account as well as the current holdings and market value of all long and short positions in the account. Statements are sent monthly for active accounts; quarterly for inactive accounts.

Statutory voting method   a voting method that requires the shareholder to divide his or her total votes equally among the issues or directorships being decided; this is the standard voting method in most corporations. (see Voting right; compare Cumulative voting method)

Step-down (up) bond another name for a variable rate bond where the interest rate on the bond is changed periodically based on current market rates. As market rates move, the interest rate "steps up" or "steps down."

Step-out well in a developmental oil and gas program, a well drilled near an adjacent oil field, thus the program is "stepping-out" from the nearby field. (see Developmental oil and gas program)

Sticky issue a new issue security that is not selling well in the primary market. As of the effective date of the underwriting, trading starts in the secondary market and the market price falls below the Public Offering Price. Thus, this issue is "stuck" on the hands of the underwriters. (compare Hot issue)

Stock a negotiable security representing ownership of a company and entitling its owner to the right to receive dividends. Both common stock and preferred stock are issued by corporations and have different characteristics and features. (see Equity security)

Stock dividend the issuance of additional shares of stock, instead of cash, as a dividend to shareholders. Stock dividends are typically "paid" by growth companies that wish to retain cash to fund future growth. Unless the company's earnings are growing rapidly, a stock dividend will dilute a company's earnings per share. (see Dividend)

Stock exchange an auction market in which exchange members meet in a central location to execute buy and sell orders for individual and institutional customers. In the United States, the largest stock exchange is the New York Stock Exchange, followed by the American Stock Exchange. In addition, there are many regional exchange floors, for example, the Chicago, Philadelphia and Pacific exchanges. These are all "First" markets. (see First market)

Stock index fund   a mutual fund that invests in a group of securities chosen to match the composition and weighting of a particular stock market index, such as the Standard and Poor's 500 Index, the New York Stock Exchange Composite Index, or the Value Line Index. Such funds track the performance of the index.

Stock option   an option contract to either buy or sell stock at a fixed price, good for a fixed time period. (see Call option, Put option)

Stock power   usually a separate document attached to a stock or bond certificate and signed by the stockholder, this is a power of attorney giving the brokerage firm the right to transfer ownership of the security to another party. In this manner, shares of stock that are held in "street" name can be transferred from buyer to seller without the transfer agent having to cancel and destroy the "old" stock certificate and issuing a "new" stock certificate to the buyer (those engraved certificates are expensive!). The original certificate is kept intact, with a new stock power completed by the buyer. (see Street name)

Stock specific risk   popularly referred to as "putting too many eggs in one basket," the risk associated with investing too much money in a single security. This is non-systematic risk. Diversification protects against this type of risk. (see Non-systematic risk, Systematic risk)

Stock split   when a company's stock price rises to a very high level, it may "split" its stock to bring the share price into a more accessible range. There can be "whole" share splits (e.g., 2:1, 3:1) or "fractional" splits (e.g., 3:2). The holder of existing shares will receive additional shares as a result of the split. The exchange where the stock trades will reduce the price of the stock proportionately on the ex date to reflect the split. Thus, the aggregate value of the investor's holdings remains unchanged.

Stockholder's equity   a synonym for net worth, the equity that remains after a company's total liabilities have been subtracted from its total assets.

Stop order   also called a stop-loss order, an order that becomes a market order to buy (buy stop) or a market order to sell (sell stop) when the security trades at a specified price, known as the stop price. Once the market goes to, or through, the stop price, the order is said to be "elected," and turns into a market order - thus the actual execution price is not known. Once elected, the order is filled "at the market." A buy stop order is placed above a stock's current market price and is executed if the market rises to, or through, that price. A sell stop order is placed below a stock's current market price and is executed if the market falls to, or through, that price. (compare Limit order, Stop-limit order)

Stop-limit order   a stop order that, instead of becoming a market order if the security trades at a specified price, becomes a limit order to buy or sell at the specified price or better. On some exchanges the stop and limit prices must be the same, while on others, the prices can be different. A buy stop-limit order is placed above a stock's current market price and is "elected" if the market rises to, or through, that price. The order then becomes a limit order to buy - so the price must meet the customer's limit for an execution. A sell stop-limit order is placed below a stock's current market price is "elected" if the market falls to, or through, that price. The order then becomes a limit order to sell - so the price must meet the customer's limit for an execution. (compare Limit order, Stop order)

Stop-loss order   another name for a stop order. (see Stop order)

Stopping stock   a Specialist courtesy function where the Specialist guarantees a price to a Floor Broker for a brief period of time, thereby allowing the Floor Broker to attempt to get a better price in the trading crowd. If the Floor Broker cannot get a better price, he or she will return to the Specialist to trade at the "stopped" price. Stopping stock is only allowed for public customer orders. (see Specialist, Floor broker)

Straddle   an option strategy involving either buying a call and a put on the same stock; or selling a call and a put on the same stock; with both options having the same strike price and expiration date. If an investor buys both the call and the put simultaneously, this is a long straddle and the investor expects the price of the stock to move either up or down. If an investor sells both the call and the put simultaneously, this is a short straddle and the investor expects the price of the stock to remain relatively flat.

Straddle order   an order to buy a call and a put; or sell a call and a put; on the same security with the same strike price and expiration. Because filling this order requires that 2 trades be completed at the same time, these orders are given priority on the CBOE floor. (see Spread priority rule)

Straight preferred   a synonym for non-convertible preferred stock.

Straight-line depreciation   a method of depreciation for tangible and real assets that pro-rates the depreciation deduction evenly over the asset's life. (compare Accelerated depreciation)

Strategic asset allocation   the determination of the percentage of assets to be placed in each asset class under an asset allocation scheme. (see Asset allocation; compare Tactical asset allocation)

Street name   industry phrase describing securities owned by an investor, but registered in the name of the brokerage firm with the transfer agent and registrar The customer is listed on the firm's records as the "beneficial owner" of the securities. It is standard industry practice for securities in a margin account to the held in street name, since these are taken by the firm as collateral for the margin loan. Thus, no customer signature on the certificates is needed for the firm to "sell out" a margin customer's stock if he fails to meet a margin call. (see Beneficial owner)

Strike price   also known as the exercise price, this is the fixed price at which stock (or other underlying instrument) can be bought or sold when a call or put option is exercised. (see Call option, Put option)

Stripped bonds   when debt securities, generally U.S. Governments, are deposited into an escrow account by a broker-dealer and securities are issued against them, representing the purchaser's participation in either the interest payments from the coupon (called IOs, for interest only); or in the principal payment (called POs, for principal only). The principal-only component functions like a zero-coupon bond. It is purchased at a discount and matures at face value. No interest payments are made during the holding period.

Various brokerage houses coined acronyms for their stripped Treasury bonds, such as CATs (Certificates of Accrual on Treasury Securities), TIGRs (Treasury Investment Growth Receipts), and COUGRs (Certificates on Government Receipts). These broker-created zero-coupon bonds are known as Treasury Receipts. these have been largely replaced by Treasury STRIPs that are directly issued by the U.S. Government. (see Treasury STRIPS)

Stripper well   in an oil and gas income program, a well that "strips out" remaining oil in the ground in a well's declining years. (see Income oil and gas program)

Structuring   the prohibited practice of breaking apart cash deposits or withdrawals into amount just under $10,000 to avoid Federal reporting of such transactions. (compare Laddering)

STRIPS   commonly used acronym for Separate Trading of Registered Interest and Principal Securities. Having witnessed the success of stripped Treasury bonds and notes created by various brokerage houses (Treasury Receipts), the U.S. Treasury decided to issue interest-only (IO) strips and principal-only (PO) strips directly on selected U.S. Government debt issues. These have largely replaced Treasury Receipts.

Student Loan Marketing Association   commonly known as Sallie Mae, SLMA is a privatized agency that buys student loans from originating lenders. Sallie Mae issues notes and bonds to finance this activity. (see Sallie Mae)

Subchapter M   the IRS regulation governing the taxation of investment companies and REITs. If a mutual fund distributes 90% or more of its net investment income to shareholders, then it is considered to be a "regulated" investment company under Subchapter M and the fund is taxed only on the retained income. Thus, the shareholders' dividend distributions are only taxed at the shareholder level. If a Real Estate Investment Trust (REIT) distributes 90% or more of its net investment income, then it is "regulated" as well. If less than the percentages specified above is distributed, then the investment company is not "regulated" and would be taxed on the full amount of its net investment income. Because of this, all investment companies maintain "regulated" status.

Subject quote in the over-the-counter market, an approximate price quote from a dealer that is "subject" to confirmation or change. (compare Nominal quote, Firm quote)

Subordinated debenture a bond whose claim on the company's assets in a liquidation is lower than that of all other bondholders. Most subordinated debentures are convertible debentures, that have been issued after the company has already sold non-convertible debentures. Any debt issued after the first level of non-convertible debt has a lower claim level on the company (is "subordinated"). To induce the new bondholders to accept this lower status, the company offers a conversion feature. (see Convertible debenture)

Subordinated loan unique to the brokerage and banking industries, part of a firm's capitalization where the lender (usually a parent company) contributes capital to the firm in the form of a subordinated loan. This type of loan specifies that the lender will be repaid after all other creditors; and there are specified conditions where the loan cannot be repaid. (see Net capital)

Subordinated royalty interest in an oil and gas program, a sharing arrangement where the general partner bears none of the costs, but defers taking a percentage of oil revenue until all costs paid by the limited partners are recovered. This is the same as a Reversionary Working Interest. (compare Disproportionate sharing arrangement, Overriding royalty interest, Net profits interest)

Subscription agreement literally, the application form to purchase a limited partnership which an investor submits detailing suitability, income and net worth information, together with a check, to the general partner. After reviewing the subscription agreement, if the general partner determines that the investor is suitable to the partnership, he signs the agreement, accepting the investor into the partnership and cashes the check. If the investor is not suitable, the check and unsigned subscription agreement are returned.

Subscription price lower than a stock's current market price, the fixed price at which a company's existing shareholders can purchase new shares during a rights offering. The discount to the current shareholders reflects the spread that an underwriter would take to sell the issue to the public. Since this is a "direct" sale of additional shares by the company to existing shareholders, there is no underwriter to pay. (see Preemptive right, Rights offering)

Subscription right the right given to a common shareholder, to have the first claim on any additional common shares that the company wishes to sell. If the company wishes to issue additional common shares, it issues subscription rights to its existing shareholders, who may exercise these rights; or may sell them in the marketplace for their value. (see Preemptive right)

Suitability the appropriateness of an investment for a customer given his or her investment profile as disclosed on the new account form. Each of the self-regulatory organizations requires that all securities recommendations made to customers be "suitable."

Sum of the years digits an accelerated depreciation method that "adds up" all of the years of an asset's depreciable life, and then "front loads" the depreciation deductions into the earlier years; and reduces the deductions in the later years; as compared to straight line depreciation. (see Accelerated depreciation)

SuperDOT originally called DOT (Designated Order Turnaround), the upgraded and consolidated version of the NYSE's automated order routing and execution system. The system currently accepts market and limit orders up to 3,000,000 shares. (see Designated Order Turnaround system)

SuperMontage introduced in 2003, NASDAQ's automated trade execution and order maintenance system for all NASDAQ issues. The system currently accepts orders for up to 999,999 shares. SuperMontage incorporated the features of the predecessor SuperSOES system. This system is now incorporated within NASDAQ's newer SingleBook system (see Single Book)

Supervisory Analyst   a FINRA/NYSE designation for an individual who has passed the Series #16 examination. This person is responsible for writing; or approving; any research reports distributed by the member firm that recommends securities.

Supply-side theory   an economic theory, popularly known as Reaganomics since it came into use during the Reagan administration, that is a mirror image of Keynesian theory. It postulates that reducing fiscal stimulus (reduction of government spending) and reducing taxes will give entrepreneurial individuals the incentive to form businesses, resulting in an expanding economy. (compare Keynesian theory, Monetarist theory)

Support level   a price level to which a stock or the market falls (and then rises from) repeatedly. Buying increases as a stock's price approaches this level, so the stock has support against further downward price moves, hence the name. If a stock's price breaks the support level, then it is believed by technical analysts that there are still sellers, without the same level of buyers, so there will be a strong downward price movement in the stock due to the excess of sellers in the market. (compare Resistance level)

Surplus capital   another name for "additional paid in capital" - that is, the amount above par value paid by a common shareholder to the company for the stock on the initial public offering.

Syndicate   a group of investment banking firms that, with the lead underwriter(s), shares in the financial responsibility and liability of offering and selling new issues to the public. Each syndicate member firm signs a document in which it agrees to share in the profit and the financial liability associated with the underwriting. (see Agreement among underwriters)

Syndicate agreement   also called the agreement among underwriters, a formal, legal agreement between the syndicate manager and each syndicate member that details the selling responsibility (including allocation of securities) and liability of each syndicate member in the underwriting of a new issue security. Such agreements can either be established as "Eastern" syndicate accounts (undivided as to selling responsibility and liability); or "Western" syndicate accounts (divided as to selling responsibility and liability). (see Syndicate, Underwriting agreement, Eastern account, Western account)

Syndicate letter   in the municipal bond market, the name for the syndicate agreement or the agreement among underwriters. Sent to and signed by each syndicate member, this letter designates the lead underwriter to manage the syndicate, allocates securities to the syndicate members, and specifies the priority in which orders will be filled. (see Syndicate agreement, Priority provisions)

Syndicate manager   also called the lead or managing underwriter, the investment banking firm that has the business relationship with the issuer of the securities. The managing underwriter forms the syndicate, drafts the syndicate agreement, acts on the syndicate's behalf, allocates the securities to each syndicate member and charges a management fee for its services. (see Agreement among underwriters)

Syndicate member   a broker-dealer who signs a syndicate agreement with the syndicate manager, and by doing so, agrees to share in the selling responsibility and liability for a new issue offering being underwritten by the syndicate. (see Syndicate agreement, syndicate manager)

Syndicator   usually the general partner in a limited partnership, this person forms the partnership, registers it with the SEC and hires "wholesalers" to market the partnership units to brokerage firms that might have customers for the program(s). These are non-managed partnership offerings. (see Non-managed offering, wholesaler)

Systematic risk   also called market risk, the risk that a market decline will adversely affect a portfolio's value. Diversification does not protect against this type of risk. (compare Non-systematic risk, Stock-specific risk)

_T_

T-bill   the common name for a U.S. Government Treasury bill, this is a money market instrument that is sold at a discount to a minimum face value of $1,000 per T-bill. Treasury bills are issued with initial 1 month, 3 month and 6 month maturities. (see Treasury bill)

TAC tranch   a Targeted Amortization Class is a CMO tranch that is buffered against prepayment risk by an associated companion tranch, but is not buffered against extension risk. (see Extension risk, Prepayment risk; compare Planned amortization class tranch, Companion tranch)

Tactical asset allocation   the permitted variation from the fixed percentage of assets to be placed in each asset class given to the asset manager under an asset allocation scheme. (see Asset allocation; compare Strategic asset allocation)

Takedown   in a new issue municipal bond offering, the discount from the public price given to a member of the syndicate. The term comes from the manager of the syndicate allowing a syndicate member to "takedown" a bond from the syndicate account at a price that is lower than the public offering price. The takedown is also referred to as the "total takedown" because it is the total of the additional takedown and the selling concession. (see Additional takedown, Selling concession, Syndicate)

Tangible asset   an asset such as machinery or equipment that is moveable. Such assets are valued on a company's balance sheet at net depreciated value. In addition to tangible assets, companies can also have intangible assets and real estate assets. (compare Intangible asset)

Tangible costs   in an oil and gas drilling program, this is the cost of purchasing tangible assets such as machinery, pumps, piping, etc. These costs must be capitalized and recovered through depreciation over the life of the oil well. (see Tangible asset; compare Intangible drilling costs)

Targeted amortization class   a CMO tranch that is buffered against prepayment risk by an associated companion tranch, but is not buffered against extension risk. (see Extension risk, Prepayment risk; compare Planned amortization class tranch; Companion tranch)

Tax and revenue anticipation note (TRAN) a short-term municipal security issued in anticipation of future tax and revenue collections that will be the source of funds to retire the note. (compare Bond anticipation note, Construction loan note, Revenue anticipation note, Tax anticipation note)

Tax anticipation note (TAN)   a short-term municipal security issued in anticipation of future tax receipts. Once the tax payments from individuals and corporations are received, the note is retired using the tax collections. (compare Bond anticipation note, Construction loan note, Revenue anticipation note, Tax and revenue anticipation note)

Tax basis   for tax purposes, the valuation of an investor's interest in a direct participation program. The adjusted tax basis is computed at the end of every year. The tax basis consists of the initial cash investment plus the assumption of any recourse financing (non-recourse financing is included in the basis for real estate only).

Each year, the basis is increased for additional cash investments; assumption of additional debt; and the distributive share of partnership income.

Each year, the basis is reduced for cash distributions; pay down of debt by the partnership; and the distributive share of partnership losses. The tax basis sets the limit for the amount of deductions an investor can take during the year. (see Direct participation program, Recourse debt, Non-recourse debt)

Tax credit   a provision of the Internal Revenue Code that allows a credit against taxes due for certain types of investment that the government wishes to encourage - e.g., low income housing or pollution control facilities.

Tax deferred   the tax-free build up of interest, dividends, and capital gains in a retirement account. These earnings are subject to taxation only when distributed or withdrawn from the account at some later (deferred) date.

Tax deferred annuity   usually called a 403(b) plan, for the section of the Internal Revenue Code that covers it, this is a pension plan specifically for certain tax-exempt, non-profit organizations - e.g., schools, municipalities, hospitals, etc. Employees are allowed to contribute to a tax-deferred annuity via payroll deduction. The amount contributed is always made with pre-tax dollars and is therefore a salary reduction for the employee, that reduces the employee's taxable income. (see 403b plan)

Tax exempt security   a term frequently used to describe a municipal bond whose interest payments are exempt from federal taxes.

Tax preference items   under IRS rules, those items that may be subject to the alternative minimum tax if, as a result of using them for a deduction, an individual's regular tax liability is reduced excessively. The four main tax preference items are: 1) accelerated depreciation amounts in excess of straight line; 2) excess percentage depletion deductions; 3) excess intangible drilling cost deductions and; 4) interest income from non-essential use, private purpose municipal bonds, such as Industrial development bonds. (see Alternative minimum tax)

Tax qualified plan   a pension or retirement plan in which the contributions are deductible against the contributor's taxable income. In effect, the contributions are made with pre-tax dollars. All earnings on the contributions are tax-deferred. When distributions begin at retirement, since none of the funds were ever taxed, the distributions from the account are 100% taxable. (compare Non-tax qualified plan)

Tax shelter   the commonly used name for a Direct Participation Program (DPP) or limited partnership.

Tax swap   a tax strategy that allows an investor to sell a municipal bond on which he or she has a capital loss and immediately reinvest the proceeds in another municipal bond. This gives the investor a tax deductible capital loss on the bond that was sold. In order for the IRS not to disallow the loss deduction under the "wash sale rule," the municipal bond that is purchased must be "different" than the one that was sold. The IRS looks at 3 determinants - the issuer, the maturity, and the coupon rate. At least 2 of the 3 must be different for the loss deduction not to be disallowed under the wash sale rule. (see Wash sale rule)

Technical analysis   research that seeks to predict the future price movement of a stock or the overall market by using price movement and volume indicators, and by using charts of a stock's past price and volume movements, to predict its future price movements. (compare Fundamental analysis)

Tenants by entireties   another name for a joint account with rights of survivorship. Each tenant 100% owns the account; if one dies, the remaining tenant(s) 100% own the account.

Tenants in common   an ownership method for a joint account where each owner (each "tenant") has a specified percentage ownership. If that person dies, his or her share goes to that person's estate. (compare Joint tenants with rights of survivorship)

Tender offer   a limited-time offer by a company to purchase its own securities or another company's outstanding securities, usually at a premium to their current market value. Such offers can be conditioned upon a minimum number of shares or bonds being tendered. If the minimum amount is not tendered, then the securities are returned to the holders and the tender offer is canceled.

Tender option   a feature of a bond that gives the holder the right to put (sell) the bond back to the issuer after a certain time. (see Puttable bond)

Term bond   a bond that is issued all at one time and that matures at one time. (compare Serial bond, Series bond)

Term repo   a repurchase agreement whose duration is longer than overnight. (see Repurchase agreement)

Thin market   also called an illiquid market, a market in which there are few buyers or sellers for a security. Such markets are characterized by low trading volumes, wide spreads, and high price volatility. (see Spread; compare Efficient market)

Third market   the trading market (secondary market) is subcategorized into the First, Second, Third, and Fourth markets. This is the order of the development of these markets in the United States. Over-the-counter firms that trade exchange listed securities do so in the Third market. Thus, so-called Third market makers compete with the exchange Specialists. (compare Specialist, First, Second, Fourth markets)

Third party   regarding brokerage accounts, the parties to the account are: First Party - Brokerage Firm; Second Party - Customer; Third Party - Anyone other than the Brokerage Firm or Customer.

Third party research report   a report prepared by an independent research firm that has no business relationship with the issuer. Member firms that prepare their own research reports must also make available to customers independent third party research reports on those issuers. Third party research reports are known as "unconflicted research reports."

Third party trading authorization   written authorization from a customer allowing a designated "Third Party" to trade the account. The authorization can either be a limited power of attorney (trading only) or a full power of attorney (trading and drawing of checks on the account are both permitted). (see Third party)

Threshold list   a list of "hard to borrow" securities with large outstanding short positions. If these securities are sold short and the seller fails to deliver on settlement, then the member firm must buy in the position no later than 10 business days after settlement (called 13 settlement days in Regulation SHO, since the rule counts from trade date instead of settlement date).

Tick   the minimum price move of a stock. On most stocks, a tick is $.01 or 1 cent.

Ticker   also called the ticker tape or the Consolidated Tape, the electronic display that continuously shows the stock symbols and prices at which each successive trade occurs during the hours that the market is open.

Time horizon   when creating a portfolio for the customer, the time period necessary to achieve the desired investment return.

Time spread   an option spread position, where simultaneously the same type of option is bought and sold with the same strike price; and different expirations. When the positions are "stacked" one above the other, there is a no difference in the strike prices, but the expirations are different - on a time line, one expiration is longer than the other, hence the name time spread. These are also called "calendar" or "horizontal" spreads. (compare Vertical spread, Diagonal spread)

Time value   the amount of an option's premium that exceeds its intrinsic value. It is the amount of money that an investor is willing to gamble that between the time an option position is established and its expiration, that the underlying security will move in the anticipated direction. (see Intrinsic value, Option)

Timing   attempting to buy or sell a security at the optimum moment in its price movement.

Timing risk   the risk that a securities transaction is not effected at the best "time" in the market. During the trading day, prices rise and fall. One experiences "timing" risk if a purchase is made when prices are high; or a sale is made when prices are low.

TIPS   abbreviation for Treasury Inflation Protection Securities, these are Treasury notes where the principal amount is indexed for inflation; however the coupon rate is fixed. If the principal amount is indexed up for inflation, then the holder will receive a higher semi-annual interest payment as well (since the interest payment is equal to the higher principal amount times the fixed interest rate).

TOD abbreviation for Transfer On Death, a new type of securities registration that allows the registered owner to specify the person in whose name the security will be transferred upon death of the owner. Thus, upon death, the security does not go into the name of the estate and bypasses probate.

Tombstone   an announcement of a public offering of securities published in financial newspapers and periodicals by the underwriters. So-called, because the announcement looks like a "tombstone," the content is legally limited by the Securities and Exchange Commission for non-exempt securities offerings so that the announcement is not considered to be overly promotional.

Total capitalization   the total long-term debt, preferred stock, and common stock that comprises a company's capital structure.

Total return   the percentage return, including both dividends and capital appreciation, on money invested in a security.

Total takedown   the largest part of the spread on a new municipal bond issue, the compensation each syndicate member receives for each bond that it sells to the public. The total takedown is the sum of the additional takedown and the selling concession. The total takedown can simply be referred to as the "takedown." (see Spread, Additional takedown, Selling concession)

TRACE   acronym for "Trade Reporting And Compliance Engine," this is FINRA/NASD's last sale reporting system for trades of non-convertible corporate bonds.

Trading authorization   written permission given by a customer allowing another person to trade that customer's account.

Trading post   the designated place on the exchange floor where a particular stock trades. A Specialist is located at each trading post and manages the trading crowd at that post. (see Specialist)

Trading unit   the standard, round-lot unit in which a security trades. For stock, warrants, and rights the standard trading unit is 100 shares. For corporate bonds, the standard trading unit is 5 bonds.

Tranch   associated with CMOs and REMICs, the grouping of a pool of mortgages into classes based on payment schedule, maturity, and/or risk. By grouping the mortgages into tranches, the issuer creates securities of differing maturities; and with differing levels of prepayment and extension risk. The word tranch comes from the French word "tranche" - for slice - since these derivative securities "slice-up" the cash flows from the underlying pass-through certificates into tranches.

Transfer agent   usually a commercial bank or trust company appointed by an issuer of a security, the transfer agent is responsible for canceling old certificates of investors who have sold shares and issuing new certificates to the purchasers of those shares. The transfer agent can also act as the paying agent, responsible for mailing dividends and other important information and documents to the shareholders. The activities of the transfer agent are overseen by the registrar. (see Registrar)

Transfer On Death   abbreviated TOD, a new type of securities registration that allows the registered owner to specify the person in whose name the security will be transferred upon death of the owner. Thus, upon death, the security does not go into the name of the estate and bypasses probate.

Treasuries   the commonly used name for U.S. Government securities.

Treasury bill   a short-term money market security issued by the U.S. Government with 6 months or less to maturity. The security is issued at a discount and matures at face value. The difference between the discounted price and the face value is the interest income paid to the holder. The Federal Reserve Board (FRB) holds weekly auctions for one-month, three-month and six-month T-bills. T-bills are issued in minimum denominations of $1,000 face value.

Treasury bond   a negotiable, long term U.S. Government security issued at par with over ten to thirty years to maturity. Interest is paid semi-annually. The minimum denomination is $1000. In late 2001, the Treasury discontinued the issuance of long bonds, but resumed issuance in February of 2006.

Treasury Inflation Protection Security   abbreviated as TIPS, these are Treasury notes where the principal amount is indexed for inflation; however the coupon rate is fixed. If the principal amount is indexed up for inflation, then the holder will receive a higher semi-annual interest payment as well (since the interest payment is equal to the higher principal amount times the fixed interest rate).

Treasury note   a negotiable, intermediate term U.S. Government security issued with two to ten years to maturity. Interest is paid semi-annually. The minimum denomination is $1000.

Treasury receipt   the generic name for a stripped U.S. Government bond created and sold by a brokerage firm. (see Stripped bond; compare Treasury STRIPS)

Treasury stock   stock that has been issued and subsequently repurchased by the issuing corporation. These shares are issued, but no longer are outstanding in the hands of the public. Corporations repurchase shares for their "Treasury" to increase reported earnings per share; and hence, the stock's price in the market. Treasury stock has no voting rights and does not receive dividends.

Treasury STRIPS   the name for stripped bonds or notes issued directly by the U.S. Government. STRIPS is an acronym for Separate Trading of Registered Interest and Principal Securities. (see Stripped bonds; compare Treasury receipt)

Trend   in technical terms, the up, down, or sideways movement of the overall market (as reflected in an average or index) or a stock's price over a period of time, usually longer than six months.

Triple-exempt security   a term used to describe a municipal bond whose interest payments are exempt from federal, state, and local taxes. Issues of territories or possessions are "triple exempt." Municipal bonds purchased by state residents are "triple exempt" in those states that have an income tax.

True interest cost   in a competitive bid underwriting where the lowest interest rate bid wins, the computation of the real interest cost to the issuer considering the time value of money. This is expressed as a single yield over the bond issue's life. (compare Net interest cost)

Trust account   a fiduciary account in which the trustee makes investment decisions for a person in keeping with the terms specified in the trust agreement. (see Fiduciary, Trustee)

Trust indenture   also called the indenture, a series of covenants or protective promises made by the issuer of a debt security to the purchasers of a debt security. Typical covenants require the issuer to make semi-annual interest payments to the bondholders and to file annual reports with the SEC (for corporate bonds).

To insure that the issuer complies with all of the terms of the covenants, an independent trustee is appointed by the issuer to protect the interests of the bondholders. The trustee is usually a commercial bank, that gives a report of its findings to the bondholders annually.

Trust Indenture Act of 1939 federal law enacted to protect corporate bondholders from harmful actions by the issuer. The Trust Indenture Act of 1939 requires issuers of non-exempt debt securities to include SEC approved protective covenants for the purchasers of the debt securities. Additionally, the issuer must appoint an independent trustee to monitor its adherence to the covenants. (see Non-exempt security, Trust indenture)

Trustee traditionally a commercial bank or trust that holds the title to, or manages securities or property, in a fiduciary account for the benefit of another person. A trustee can also be an individual or a brokerage firm. (see Trust account)

Twenty (20) day cooling off period mandated under the Securities Act of 1933, the period of time following the filing of a registration statement with the SEC, during which time the issuer and underwriter(s) are prohibited from selling the issue, advertising the issue, recommending the purchase of the issue, and soliciting orders to buy the issue. During the "cooling-off period," the SEC reviews the filing for "full and fair disclosure."

Twenty (20) G.O. Bond Index a yield index compiled by the Bond Buyer each week, consisting of 20 selected municipal general obligation bonds, rated A or better, with 20 years to maturity. It is a reference used by municipal underwriters to set the coupon rate on a municipal new issue. (compare Revdex)

Two-dollar Broker also known as independent broker, a New York Stock Exchange member who executes orders for any member firm in any security and is paid a commission for his or her services. There are a relative handful of these firms, and they mainly execute orders for retail firms whose floor brokers are either too busy; or where the retail firm wants to disguise its trading. The name comes from the $2 commission that these firms used to receive for each round-lot execution. (compare Floor broker)

_U_

U.S. Savings bond   non-negotiable Series EE bonds issued by the U.S. Government. These are redeemable with the U.S. Treasury. (see Series EE bond)

UQDF   acronym for UTP (Unlisted Trading Privileges) Quote Data Feed, this is the quote source for all market centers quoting NASDAQ-listed issues. These quote sources include NASDAQ market markers, exchange Specialists trading NASDAQ issues under a UTP plan, and ECNs. (see UTP, ECN)

UTP   acronym for Unlisted Trading Privileges, any exchange is now permitted to trade any stock listed on any other exchange or NASDAQ, even though the stock is not listed on that exchange. Thus, the NYSE can trade issues only listed on NASDAQ via a "so-called" UTP plan; and NASDAQ can trade issues only listed on the NYSE via a UTP plan.

Uncovered option   also called a naked option, a term used to describe a short call or short put position in which the writer is unprotected against the maximum possible loss. (see Short call, Short put; compare Covered option)

Underwriter   also known as an investment banker, a brokerage firm that assists an issuer of a new security in setting the offering price and in marketing the securities to the public.

Underwriter's concession   that portion of the underwriting spread which the managing underwriter concedes or gives to the syndicate members in a corporate securities underwriting for each new issue security they sell directly to the public. (see Spread)

213

Underwriting agreement the formal written agreement between the issuer and underwriter, that is signed just prior to the commencement of sale of the issue. In this document, the final public offering price, spread, and net proceeds to the issuer are established; And the underwriter agrees to sell the issuer's securities to the public, either on a firm commitment or best efforts basis. (see Firm commitment underwriting, best efforts underwriting)

Underwriting spread the total compensation received by the brokerage firm participating in the underwriting and sale of a new issue security, this is the difference between the Public Offering Price and the price paid to the issuer. The "spread" is broken down into components earned by each participant in the underwriting.

For a corporate new issue, the spread components typically consist of the management fee, the underwriter's concession, the selling concession, and (perhaps) the reallowance. (see Management fee, Underwriter's concession, Selling concession, Reallowance)

For a municipal new issue, the spread components typically consist of the management fee, the additional takedown, and the selling concession. (see Management fee, Additional takedown, Total takedown, Selling concession)

Undivided account the same as an Eastern syndicate account, a syndicate agreement in which each member has technically unlimited selling responsibility and unlimited liability. Typical for municipal underwritings, each member takes a percentage of the offering. This percentage does not limit sales by the member. However, if securities remain unsold out of the total syndicate account, each member is liable for that percentage of all unsold securities. Thus, each member's liability is affected by the performance of all other syndicate members. (compare Western syndicate, Divided syndicate)

Uniform Gifts to Minors Act adopted in each state, UGMA details the requirements for opening and operating a custodian account for the benefit of a minor (child). This Act has been replaced by UTMA - Uniform Transfers to Minors Act - in most states. (see Custodian account)

Uniform Transfers to Minors Act   adopted in each state, UTMA details the requirements for opening and operating a custodian account for the benefit of a minor (child). This Act replaces UGMA in all but 2 states, with the major differences being that UTMA permits more than securities to be gifted; and allows a transfer age up to age 21 to be specified by the custodian. (see Custodian account)

Uniform Securities Act   adopted in each state, these are the state "blue sky" laws that require registration of securities, broker-dealers and agents in that state. (see Blue-sky laws)

Unissued stock   unissued stock is that which is authorized in the company's charter but has never been issued to the public. It is not the same as Treasury stock, which consists of shares that have been issued, and subsequently repurchased, by the company.

Unit investment trust (UIT)   one of the three types of investment companies defined in the Investment Company Act of 1940. A UIT is organized not as a corporation, but as a trust which issues units (called shares of beneficial interest) representing an undivided interest in a portfolio of securities. UITs can either be "fixed" or "participating." In a fixed UIT, the trust establishes a portfolio that never changes. The portfolio eventually self-liquidates. In a participating UIT, a holding company buys open-end management company (mutual fund) shares. Investors buy units of the holding company. (see Fixed UIT, Participating UIT)

Unit refund life annuity   an annuity option where, if the annuitant dies before receiving the full investment value of the annuity contract, the remainder is refunded to his or her estate. (compare Joint and last survivor annuity, Life annuity, Life annuity with period certain)

Unlimited tax bond   a municipal General Obligation bond with no limit on the amount of taxes that can be levied in order to pay off the bond. This is the normal type of G.O. pledge, that is, a bond backed by faith, credit, and unlimited taxing power. (see General obligation bond; compare Limited tax bond))

Unlisted securities   virtually synonymous with smaller over-the-counter stocks and almost all bonds, a term used to describe any stock or other security that is not listed on an exchange or on the NASDAQ Stock Market.

Unmanaged direct participation program offering   a tax shelter limited partnership security that is offered on a best efforts basis by a "wholesaler" who sells the units strictly on an agency basis for the sponsor. (see Limited partnerships, Sponsor, Wholesaler)

Unqualified legal opinion   sometimes called a clean legal opinion, the written opinion of the bond counsel that no contingencies exist that could affect a new municipal bond's legality, validity, and tax exempt status. Thus, there are no "qualifications" to the opinion. (compare Qualified legal opinion)

Unrealized gain   the profit resulting from an increase in the value of a long security position or a decrease in the value of a short security position that is still being held. There is no taxation of the gain until the position is liquidated.

Unsecured bond   a bond backed by the full faith and credit of the issuer. There are no specific assets or property pledged to back the bond. Corporate debentures and municipal general obligation bonds are examples of unsecured bonds. (compare Secured bond)

Unsponsored ADR   an American Depositary Receipt in which the corporation that issued the stock in the foreign country is not involved in the issuance of the ADRs in the United States. Usually a bank handles all the details of the issuance. (see American Depositary Receipt; compare Sponsored ADR)

Unsystematic risk   another term for non-systematic or stock-specific risk, this is the risk that can be diversified out of a portfolio by adding a greater number of securities to the portfolio, until its composition matches the "market." This leaves the portfolio with only "systematic" risk - that is, market risk that cannot be diversified away. (compare Systematic risk)

Uptrend the upward movement of a stock's price, or of the market as a whole as measured by an average or index, over a period of time. (compare Downtrend)

_V_

Value investing   the selection of equity investments based on finding undervalued issues using fundamental analysis. (see Fundamental analysis; compare Growth investing)

Value Line Index   a geometrically weighted index consisting of some 1,700 selected issues that are on the NYSE, AMEX, and over-the-counter markets. These are the securities that are followed and rated by the Value Line Investment Survey.

Variable annuity   a unit trust form of an investment company where an insurance company sells an annuity in which the amount of the periodic payments to the investor (called the annuitant) will vary with the value of the mutual funds held in the underlying portfolio. The underlying portfolio is termed the "separate account," since these investments are segregated from the insurance company's general investment account. These are redeemable securities that do not trade. Variable annuities are a non-exempt security under the Securities Act of 1933 and must be sold with a prospectus. (see Annuity, Non-exempt security, Unit investment trust)

Variable rate demand note   short term municipal notes where the issuer resets the interest rate every six months, based upon some defined measure, such as the 6-month Treasury Bill interest rate. At the reset date, the owner can either continue to hold the note at the new interest rate; or can redeem the note with the issuer at par. Thus, the interest rate on the note varies; and the note is payable upon demand of the holder at each reset date.

Velocity of money   the frequency with which money changes hands once it is injected into the economy by the Federal Reserve. The velocity of money increases when economic activity increases and tends to decrease during periods of recession. The velocity is also determined by Federal Reserve actions on how long banks can take to clear funds that are deposited - shorter clearance times speed up the velocity.

Venture capital   money invested in a new, unproven and risky business or enterprise.

Vertical merger   a merger of 2 companies in different businesses. For example, the merger of an automobile manufacturer and a tire manufacturer is a vertical merger. (compare Horizontal merger)

Vertical spread   an option spread position, where simultaneously the same type of option is bought and sold with different strike prices; and the same expiration. When the positions are "stacked" one above the other, there is a vertical difference in the strike prices, hence the name. These are also called "price" spreads. There are 4 types of vertical spreads - bull call spreads, bear call spreads, bull put spreads, and bear put spreads. (compare Horizontal spread, Diagonal spread)

Vesting   a period of time over which an employer's contributions to a pension plan becomes the property of the employee. Under ERISA, most pension plans vest over five years, at a rate of 20% per year. (see ERISA)

Visible supply   also called the 30-day Visible Supply, the total dollar amount of long-term tax-exempt municipal bonds being issued in the primary market over the next 30 days via competitive bid or negotiated underwriting. The measure does not include short term municipal notes. Found in the Bond Buyer, this is a measure of new issue supply and is one of the references used to determine the coupon rate on a new long term municipal issue. (see Bond buyer)

Volatility   the frequency with which the price of security moves up and down. The larger and more frequent the movement, the greater the volatility of the security. (see Alpha, Beta)

Volume   the total number of shares traded in a given period of time.

Voting right the right of a common shareholder to vote to elect the members of the company's Board of Directors; and to vote on any matters that would affect the shareholder's ownership interest. (see Statutory voting method, Cumulative voting method)

Voting trust a trust, usually having a maximum life of 10 years, established to control the voting shares of a corporation.

Voting trust certificate (VTC) a negotiable certificate, issued by a trustee, that represents the deposit of the securities into the trust and the relinquishing of all voting privileges. Although the investor continues to receive all other benefits of ownership, such as dividends, only the trust has the right to vote. The certificate trades in the secondary markets.

W

WAII   abbreviation for when, as, and if issued, a phrase which indicates that a security is trading in the market that has been authorized for issuance, but that it is not yet physically available for delivery (e.g., the printed certificates are not yet ready).

Warrant   usually attached to a new bond or preferred stock issue as a "sweetener" to increase the issue's marketability. a warrant gives the holder the right to buy a stated amount of common stock at a specified price. This specified price is initially higher than the stock's current market price. For the warrant to have value, the market price of the stock must rise above the exercise price of the warrant. Currently issued warrants have a limited life; however, in the past, some companies have issued "perpetual" warrants that have no expiration date. Warrants trade separately in the market from the security to which they were originally attached.

Wash sale rule   an IRS rule that disallows a capital loss resulting from the sale of a security if the customer has bought the same or a substantially similar security during the period starting 30 days before the sale until 30 days after the sale. In addition to buying the same stock, actions that result in the investor owning a "substantially similar" security include buying a call, right, or warrant on the same security, buying a security convertible into the one that was sold at a loss, as well as writing deep in-the-money puts on the security sold at a loss. (compare Tax swap)

Wasting asset   a security that becomes worthless on a predetermined expiration date. Rights, standard warrants, and options are securities that are wasting assets.

Weighting   the method for determining the worth of each company's stock relative to the value of an overall index.

Western syndicate   a syndicate agreement in which each member is only responsible and liable for selling the fixed amount of the issue it is allocated. Each member's liability is unaffected by the performance of the other syndicate members. This is known as a divided syndicate, because the offering is "divided up" among the syndicate members (see Syndicate; compare Eastern syndicate)

When issued   the short form of when, as, and if issued, a phrase which indicates that a security is trading in the market that has been authorized for issuance, but that it is not yet available for physical delivery (e.g., the printed certificates are not yet ready).

When issued security   a security that is sold to the public and trades in the market before the physical certificates are available for distribution.

White's Rating   a service that rates the marketability risk associated with a municipal issue using a scale from 0 to 1, with 0 denoting an unmarketable issue and 1 a most liquid issue. Marketability risk is inherent in the municipal market, since the marketplace is so fragmented (it is a state by state market). Note that White's is no longer in business, but may still be tested. (see Marketability risk)

Wholesaler   in a non-managed offering of a limited partnership, an independent agent or employee of the syndicator who sells partnership interests to the public through FINRA/NASD member firms. A wholesaler earns a portion of the spread for each of these sales. (see Non-managed offering, Syndicator)

Wildcat well   in an exploratory oil and gas program, a well drilled far away from an existing field. (The term comes from the first Texas "wildcatters" of the early 1900s who found the very first oil reserves. (see Exploratory oil and gas program)

Wilshire Index   considered the broadest measure of the activity and movement of the overall stock market, this index consists of about 7,000 issues of companies headquartered in the United States that trade on the NYSE, AMEX, and on NASDAQ. Note that the index originally started with 5,000 issues in the mid 1970s, but has been expanded as the listings in the markets have grown.

Workable quote   in the municipal bond market, a bid price at which a dealer is likely to buy bonds from dealer who wishes to sell. The dealer soliciting the "workable" is trying to execute a customer's order to sell municipal bonds, and is collecting likely prices at which other dealers would buy the bonds. After "shopping around" for workables, the selling dealer will go back to the buying dealer who gave the best "workable" to nail down a firm bid for the bonds.

Workout quote   in the over-the-counter market, an approximate price range which the dealer will use to work out a firm quote in a reasonable amount of time.

Worksheet   the form used by an underwriter in a competitive bid municipal bond offering to formulate a bid - i.e., write the scale. The underwriter obtains the worksheets from the Bond Buyer. (see Bond buyer, Scale)

Wrap account   a brokerage account where all customer services are "wrapped" into 1 account, including trade executions, investment management and portfolio allocation; with an annual fee typically based on a percentage of total assets invested with the firm. This is considered to be an "advisory product," so persons selling "wrap" accounts must be registered as both sales representatives and investment adviser representatives in most states (Series #63 and Series #65 license).

Writer   the seller of an option contract, synonymous with being "short" the contract. (compare Holder)

Writing the scale   the process of formulating a competitive bid on a proposed municipal bond issue offering where the lead underwriter and the syndicate set the yield and price on each maturity of a serial bond issue. (see Scale)

XYZ

XMI   the symbol for stock index option on the Major Market Index, traded on the American Stock Exchange.

Yankee bond   a bond, denominated in dollars, that is issued in the U.S. by a foreign corporation. This bond would be registered with the SEC, since it is a non-exempt issue. (see Non-exempt security)

Yellow sheets   published daily by the National Quotations Bureau, these sheets show the bid and asked prices of corporate bonds that trade OTC. The sheets get their name from the color of the paper on which they are printed.

Yield   the percentage or rate of return that an investor earns on capital invested in a security or in a portfolio of securities.

Yield auction   the commonly used name for the issuance or sale of U.S. Government securities via competitive bid auction without an underwriter. Bids at this auction are made in terms of interest rates (yields) instead of prices, with the lowest interest rates winning. Yield auctions are conducted weekly by the Federal Reserve acting for the U.S. Treasury.

Yield curve   a graph, with a vertical axis depicting the yield and a horizontal axis representing years to maturity, that depicts the yields of bonds with similar quality but different maturities. The shape of the yield curve can be ascending (normal), descending, flat, or humped. The shape is dependent on investor expectations for future interest rate levels, actions of the Federal Reserve to tighten or loosen credit, and the supply and demand for debt issues in each maturity segment of the curve. (see Ascending yield curve, Descending yield curve, Flat yield curve, Hump shaped yield curve)

Yield spread   the difference in yield between 2 types of debt securities. Typically, there is a standard relationship that exists creating the "spread;" an unusual narrowing or widening of the spread can indicate changing economic conditions. A typical yield spread comparison is the yield of U.S. Government securities to "AAA" rated corporate bonds. Generally, high quality corporate bonds yield 1% more than equivalent maturity U.S. Government bonds. If the economy appears headed for recession, investors sell corporate bonds and buy U.S. Governments for safety. This drives the price of corporates down relative to governments; thus corporate yields rise relative to governments; and the yield spread "widens" to, say 2% from the usual 1%.

Yield to call   the rate of return that a bond would provide if the investor held it only to a closer call date rather than to maturity. This calculation takes into account the compounding of semi-annual interest payments; the discount or premium price of the bond at the time it was purchased; and any premium that the issuer would pay for calling the bond before its maturity date. (compare Yield to maturity, Yield to Put)

Yield to maturity   the rate of return that a bond would provide if the investor held it to its maturity date. This calculation takes into account the compounding of semi-annual interest payments, as well as the discount or premium price of the bond at the time it was purchased. (compare Yield to call, Yield to Put)

Yield to put   the rate of return that a bond would provide if the investor held it to the first date that the put feature could be exercised, rather than to maturity. This calculation takes into account the compounding of semi-annual interest payments, the discount or premium price of the bond at the time it was purchased, and any gain or loss resulting from exercising the put feature. (compare Yield to maturity, Yield to call)

Zero-coupon bond   a bond that makes no semi-annual interest payments over its life. Instead, the security is issued at a deep discount and matures at face value. The difference between the discounted purchase price and the face value is the interest income on the bond.